What they're saying about this series and the authors...

The West Orange Chamber of Commerce is proud to be connected with Mike)'Keefe, Scott Girard and Marc Price of **Expert Business Advice**. Their dyamic presentations, intellectual wealth, and unique insight into small business ave helped numerous Chamber members take their businesses to the next level."

Krista Compton Carter, IOM

West Orange Chamber of Commerce Vice President

"Over the years, Scott Girard has provided my business and me with invaluable guidance and direction. He is a true visionary."

David Van Beekum, Owner

DB Tech Design, Inc.

"I've had the pleasure of working with Michael O'Keefe on many projects over he years. His ability to evaluate situations, identify competitive advantage opporunities and implement well thought-out strategic plans is second to none."

Jim Costello

Director of Project Management

Marriott International Design & Construction Management

"Marc Price is a business builder! I have seen him start with a blank piece of paper and create a million dollar business for a financial education online application and service. He is a natural network builder and relationship marketer who works hard, is very creative, and who usually surpasses all objectives for sales, service, and market share growth. You want Marc on your team if your goal is to grow your brand and increase top and bottom lines."

Mike Schiano, MA, CRHC, CPFC

Information and Technology Services

"As an entrepreneur and owner of Professional Accounting Services, I retained Mark Moon to handle complex tax and legal issues for my business. He consistently meets short deadlines with thoughtful counsel, keeping larger business objectives in mind and putting lesser issues in proper perspective. Mark understood our needs quickly and his advice has been very effective. His knowledge and broad range of experience in business, negotiations, and intellectual property allowed me to move forward, confident that I had the appropriate legal protection in place.

Anne Nymark

President, Professional Accounting Services

"Business matters require expert guidance and Mark Moon is an excellent choice. As my legal counsel, Mark was a key factor in continuing the success of my business. I could not have asked for a better attorney to be a part of my team. I strongly recommend Mark for any and all needs in corporate and business law."

Deger Saner

Independent Marketing Professional

"As our businesses attorney, Mark Moon has been an integral part of our business sustainability and growth. The downturn in the housing market put a tremendous burden on our company. With Mark's help we were able to survive, then thrive. By adding stronger contracts and Mark's general business consulting we were able to regrow our business on a stronger foundation. Whether we want to bounce an idea off him or are looking to add some real estate, he is here for us with no sugar coating to give us good legal and business advice. I would recommend Mark to any business owner."

Brian McKenzie

Vice President of Sales

McCabinet, Inc.

"Mark Moon has been an invaluable resources, from our first consultation prior to starting the business through the continuing advice and assistance he and his firm provide. Our business would not be where it is today without him. I strongly recommend him. "

Eugene Meisenheimer

CEO

Mocomei Services, Inc.

BUSINESS LAW BASICS

CRASH COURSE for ENTREPRENEURS

BUSINESS LAW BASICS

Learn What You Need in Two Hours

Scott L. Girard, Jr., Michael F. O'Keefe,
Mark A. Price, and Mark R. Moon, Esq.

Series Editor: Scott L. Girard, Jr.

A Crash Course for Entrepreneurs—From Expert Business Advice

Starting a Business

Sales and Marketing

Managing Your Business

Business Finance Basics

Business Law Basics

International Business

Business Plans

Time and Efficiency

Franchising

Social Media Basics

Web-Based Business

Supplemental Income

Copyright © 2014, Scott L. Girard, Jr., Michael F. O'Keefe, and Mark A. Price

ISBN: 978-90-77256-39-8

The Expert Business Advice trademark is owned by Expert Business Advice, LLC and is used under license. www.expertbusinessadvice.com

Disclaimer: While every attempt has been made to verify the accuracy of information in this book as it goes to press, the authors and publisher cannot guarantee its future accuracy. Please consult competent expert advice before taking decisions in response to the advice herein.

Distributed by Career Press, Inc., 220 West Parkway, Unit 12, Pompton Plains, NJ 07444, U.S.A., www.careerpress.com

D/2014/9797/2

Printed in the United States of America

20 19 18 17 16 15 14 13 12 11 10 9 8 7 6 5 4 3 2

Cover design: Bradford Foltz

Text design: Softwin

To my wife, Marguerite and my children,
Madison, Meredith and Matthew

Contents

Foreword

YOU CAN SPOT ENTREPRENEURS easily when they talk about their businesses and dreams. Their passion and fascination with their business—and others' businesses—is remarkable. When I met Scott, Mike and Marc, I knew before they told me about the many businesses they've collectively started that these were talented, insightful, seasoned entrepreneurs. We quickly agreed to develop the Crash Course for Entrepreneurs together. For this volume in the series, we invited Mark Moon to contribute his considerable legal expertise, as both entrepreneur and attorney.

The aim of this series is to give you high-level overviews of the critical things you need to know and do if you want to start (or you're already running) your own business. In a two-hour read. Of course, there's much more to know about every topic covered, but we believe that what you'll read here will give you the framework for learning the rest. A Resources section and a Glossary will ensure you can ground yourself in the essentials. And www.expertbusinessadvice.com, the co-authors' website, offers expanded support for entrepreneurs that is updated daily.

Entrepreneurs vary widely in what they want to do. Your dream may be to start a very small, one-person service, perhaps doing home maintenance or day care or accounting from your home. You may have developed or discovered a high-tech breakthrough that will need years of testing and dozens or hundreds of people to bring to market. This book sees the intrinsic value and challenges of both styles of business. It will definitely help you make the most of your opportunity, whatever its scale.

As we mentioned above, Mark Moon joins Scott, Mike and Marc as our subject matter expert for this volume. He is a founding and the Managing Partner of the Moon Law Group, P.L., a full-service law firm. Over the years he has helped many start-ups and small businesses to make smart legal plans and decisions. Thanks to both his professional training and his day-to-day work with clients and managing the business of his firm, Mark fully understands the many, varied business issues any entrepreneur must face daily.

You'll find the initials of each author at the end of each section. Here's a brief word from each of them.

I remember when I fully understood what our series of books should accomplish. We had recently decided that we wanted to write a series of books for people only moderately familiar with entrepreneurship and business. Multitudes of books already exist on basic levels of business practices and procedures. We knew that writing another one of those books wouldn't really serve anyone or change anything, no matter how well written it was.

On the morning that I "got it," I was drinking coffee and reading the news; the television was on in the background. I glanced up and saw a commercial for a foreign language software program in which, instead of learning by simply repeating vocabulary, the student is culturally immersed in the language, holistically surrounded with concepts of all manner of things applicable to the subject. In short, they don't list facts and terms and call it teaching—they show the student a vast array of information, on a multitude of levels, allowing her to bathe in knowledge.

I knew then that instead of presenting a bunch of facts that we think you should know about business, we should take a more holistic approach and help you immerse yourself in business thinking. Our method is most effective if you read this book cover to cover, skipping nothing. If you reach a section and either think it doesn't address your needs, or you think you know everything there is to know about the subject, read it anyway. It'll only take a minute—that's why the sections are not lengthy. It will enlighten and organize your thinking, either way. You'll see important concepts woven through various discussions, as they holistically fit in.

If you're hoping to read a book and immediately become the world's greatest businessperson, this book isn't for you. If your goal, however, is to quickly understand and feel familiar with the basics of business law, as one of your first stepping stones to greatness, we believe that our book has no rival.

I sincerely hope that this book will not only increase your understanding of entrepreneurship and basic business law, but that it also gives you pleasure and satisfaction as you learn the key principles and language of business.

Scott L. Girard, Jr.

When we sat down and decided to take on the daunting task of writing a series of books for entrepreneurs and small business owners, I cringed. I thought, "How can we ever reduce our advice and experiences to writing? And how can we cover it all—can we fit it into a book?"

Either way, we decided to get started, so each of us began drafting sections related to our respective specialties and work experience. Only as the initiative continued did I discover a certain passion for sharing my advice in a personal way, trying to convey how it felt to go places, negotiate situations, and experience new things, both good and bad, in the course of starting businesses.

I take the same approach with business as I did with competitive sailing with my father when I was a kid. It's all about constant adjustment. You don't just rig the boat and go. It's about looking around, reading the wind, and predicting shifts and changes before they happen—just like understanding the external forces that affect a business or industry. While doing so, you are constantly looking around at other boats, just like you'd do benchmarking against other competitors in business—analyzing their speed and angle and comparing it to your own. Most often, what gets a boat (or business) ahead isn't some significant advantage; it's the inches or degrees of adjustment and the teamwork that generates the results. If you can point just a little higher or generate just a little more boat speed, it can make all the difference in the world—just like in business. If the organization can run just a little bit more efficiently, demonstrate better teamwork, identify the out-in-front opportunities, and not "just kind of want it" but rather, do anything to win, it will be the most likely to succeed.

I hope that this book will capture your interest, provide valuable information, and share an interesting perspective into the world of entrepreneurial business and business law.

Mike F. O'Keefe

Everyone has heard the phrase "Knowledge is Power." I would have it read "Information is Power," for a couple of reasons.

We live in an age of instant information about every facet of our lives. We can receive news, on-demand weather and traffic reports, sports scores, social media happenings, and stock market updates. And yet, we forget much of this information within moments of receiving it, as new reports and updates are constantly replacing the data we were just beginning to process.

Most generic information travels fast these days. On the other hand, some information is meant to stay with us for a while, if not forever. And with that in mind, Scott, Mike and I set out to write a series of books to deliver lasting, valid information for entrepreneurs and small business owners.

Our passion for success in business and in life lies behind every page we write. As life-long, serial entrepreneurs, we have always taken the approach of surrounding ourselves with information, ideas and viewpoints from countless sources to support our efforts in constructing our next project. That information, when reliable and trustworthy, can and will be used over and over for repeated success. So, in essence, information is power, when applied over time.

Our series of books represents the hard work, research and application of numerous business philosophies, ideas and viewpoints. You will find rock-solid information that can be applied now…and later. It's information that can be shared, and then referred to as a refresher down the road, if needed. Our goal was to deliver information and advice that is relevant, smart and timely. We hope these fresh, contemporary approaches to the fundamentals of business finance will get you, and keep you, at the top of your game.

The way forward begins here…

Marc A. Price

When Scott, Mike and Marc first approached me about writing this book, I was intrigued, but I admit I had some questions. Why me? How could anyone produce a two-hour read on business law basics?

While discussing the proposal with them and with some of my clients and peers, they reminded me why they choose to work with me and continue to recommend my firm to others. First, I have the unique business experience of being both an entrepreneur and an attorney. I started and operated businesses (and consulted with several attorneys!) before entering law school. Today, we tailor the legal services our firm offers in ways that eliminate the fears of small business owners and individuals. I know how they think; I've been there—and am a founder and managing partner today.

Also, I've had a lot of practice in explaining the law. We focus all of our consultations and ongoing representation on the premise of informed decision making by our clients. We educate our clients so that they may fully understand the legal and business ramifications of the decisions they make. This is an unusual practice, but it works. Many of my clients are amazed by the process and their long-term successes.

Finally, I run my law firm like a traditional small business. We focus on areas like customer service, efficiency of operations and long-term customer relations in addition to the traditional practice of law. I realized that these qualities uniquely position me to contribute to this book.

My legal training at first made me hesitant to attempt to break down and simplify complex issues. You easily can pick a random paragraph from this book and expand it to 300 pages, with cases and legal citations. But the concept of a Crash Course for Entrepreneurs book appealed to me, with its goal of making its readers conversant with key terms and principles. The challenge of connecting with you, the reader, and sharing what are indeed complex concepts through everyday language and simple examples is familiar to me. It's what I try to do every day with my client consults. As I wrote, I kept recalling a favorite quote from Warren Buffet: "The business schools reward difficult complex behavior more than simple behavior, but simple behavior is more effective."

I have tried to write this book with all of these principles in mind and to lay out the most complex concepts simply and straightforwardly. I hope this book will give you the tools you need for the ultimate success in your business enterprises, whether that is through your own knowledge or knowing when to contact a good attorney.

Mark R. Moon, Esq.

We all hope this book supports the fire and drive you feel now as you think about starting or confront the realities of running your own business and meeting its challenges, legal or otherwise, day to day. And we wish you success.

Kathe Grooms
Managing Director, Nova Vista Publishing

A Start-Up and the Law: A Three-Year Scenario

Event	Kind of Legal Advice or Service Involved
Year 1	
Decide now is the time to start up.	Pick an attorney. Get corporate structure and partnership advice, necessary papers. Sign attorney on as retained external legal advisor.
Business plan.	Review for any legal risks, list legal advisor in company team section of the plan.
Rent a corner café.	Rental agreement defining what the owner will do to upgrade and redecorate. Bonds for construction workers. Parking and wine permits from city council.
Pick a name, plan and print menus, hire waiter.	Possible trademark work. Contract with copy shop printer and other vendors to get good prices based on guaranteed purchases per year. Get advice on any hiring, pay, work rules needed.
Grand opening.	Social networking—introduce Maria and Paulo to attorney's dinner guests, a banker and a client who plans special events for corporations and individuals.
Year-end taxes.	Legal filings.
Year 2	
Hire chef to handle heavy demand.	Non-compete agreement re Paulo's secret spaghetti sauce ingredient.
Chef cuts fingertip off when slicing veal.	Health and safety policies, insurance claim denied and appealed.
Kitchen inspection.	Appear at City Hall to explain why bread got moldy and customers got sick. Compensation to customers (product liability).
Fire chef for telling another chef about secret sauce ingredient.	Labor law. Advice re patent law and low benefit of patenting secret spaghetti sauce ingredient.
Year-end taxes.	Legal filings.
Year 3	
Expand to second café across town, via franchise.	Franchise agreement, rental agreement, grand opening, etc. as in Year 1.
Former chef opens competing café using Paulo's secret spaghetti sauce ingredient.	Get cease and desist order and try for damages for lost business and unfair business practice.
Discord and stress between Maria and Paulo leads to divorce.	Business dissolution and divorce agreement. Each of them gets one café under separate new names and agrees to use but also to protect info on the secret spaghetti sauce ingredient.
Paulo takes on new partner who owns a produce farm.	New partnership agreement including supply of produce. Labor law regarding farm workers. Immigration law regarding their paperwork.
Maria specializes in events (thanks to contact in Year 1) and opens a chain of cafes that eventually goes international.	International business law issues.
Paulo and new partner get fed up with the long hours and strain of the café and farm and agree to sell both to an entrepreneur with a dream…	Sale of business agreement.
Postscript: what's the secret ingredient?	Grape jelly!

Introduction

*In this scenario of the first three years of a business,
we serve up a light-hearted look at how it intersects
with the world of business law.*

YOU DON'T NEED A CORPORATE ATTORNEY every day, but as a small business owner or start-up entrepreneur, you'll run into situations from time to time where consulting with one is definitely necessary. Consider the scenario opposite, covering the first three years of a business's life.

Maria and Paulo have dreamt about starting a little Italian café for years. Paulo is a great cook, and Maria loves making people feel welcome and happy. He'll run the kitchen while she works the 20 little tables out front. They agree to be equal partners in the new venture.

As you'll see, "things happen," and in surprisingly many moments, they need legal advice.

We open this book with this scenario to give you a moment to reflect on the various ways in which you can benefit from legal counsel. Our goal is neither to push you into an attorney's office nor to pretend this book is a do-it-yourself law manual. But we believe your sense of when to talk with your attorney, your ability to ask intelligent questions, and your foundation for making good choices will improve as you read on.

The book is set up in a logical flow, with basics up front; then chapters on starting up, operating, growing and exiting a business; and finally tips for avoiding trouble and for doing international business. We are pleased that the book is available worldwide, so we want to point out that our own business experience is a blend of U.S. and international activity. We know that vocabulary and practices vary from place to place, so if you need to, check what we describe and adapt it to your locality. We hope our experience and insights will guide you to a successful future in your business.

CHAPTER I

What Is Business Law?

Do I Need a Lawyer?

The short answer? You bet!

LAWYERS SOMETIMES GET A BAD RAP. We've all heard our share of lawyer jokes. But as an entrepreneur, you'd be silly to buy into the common stereotypes that have accumulated over centuries. Smart entrepreneurs view attorneys as a valuable resource and one of their most significant allies in starting, growing, protecting and ensuring the successful lives of their businesses.

So what are lawyers good for?

Lawyers are good for a number of things, some of which are less obvious than others. Most people think of attorneys when they are contemplating starting a new business, when creating and reviewing contracts, and of course when they need protecting in the event of a legal issue.

However, there are many more duties a business owner can ask an attorney to handle. The possibilities are almost endless, but include these:

- Monitoring and fulfilling ongoing filing requirements, depending on what type of business you have

- Ensuring compliance with any regulations that apply to your company

- Keeping you current on product liability developments and coverage

- Serving as your Registered Agent, which means they act as a designated recipient of all Service of Process (SOP) communications in the event of a legal action or lawsuit

- Preparing fundraising documents, such as private placement memoranda

- Ensuring your Intellectual Property protection, which can be extremely important if you or your business have a unique idea or product not currently available in the marketplace

- Conducting litigations, making real estate and equipment arrangements, etc.

- Making collections on invoices, drawing up template agreements your non-legal associates can use with proper training and guidelines

- Scanning trade news and alerting you to any emerging issues you need to anticipate

- Helping you set up document and data archiving and protection resources

- Connecting you with useful business contacts in the attorney's practice or even social circles

If you are still dubious, just ask self-employed and small business owners what kinds of support they get from their attorneys. You'll hear some amazing stories.

But I can't afford an attorney. I need that money for more important things!

Yes, legal costs can mount up, but it's often true that those sums are a fraction of what you could pay or lose without the benefit of competent legal advice. You are probably gifted and well grounded in your core business. Don't assume that that naturally qualifies you to be a legal expert, even in your own industry sector's affairs.

And if your start-up is the first one you've launched, you may learn a lot from your seasoned attorney's broad view of other small businesses and their successes and failures. You may have many governmental responsibilities to fulfill as well: Depending on what type of business you are currently operating or starting, you may owe information to various units of government and others. You cannot afford to make mistakes through ignorance or inexperience in these areas.

But what are the risks of skipping steps usually handled by attorneys?

There are a number of common business mistakes made by foolish entrepreneurs. One common error is selecting the wrong type of business entity or filing status for a new business. This mistake can end in much more labor-intensive document preparation and filings, unnecessary expenses, complicated and time-consuming reporting requirements and potentially unpleasant tax implications.

Another common mistake hurts business owners who improperly formulate employment, confidentiality and non-disclosure agreements. These documents, more than any others, can prevent associates, among others, from "biting the hand that feeds them." That hand is yours.

- Imagine hiring and training someone who then decides she will go out on her own in your neighborhood and start a competing business.

- Or what if you hire a salesperson whom you pay to build a large book of business and contacts, but who then tries to blackmail you into paying him more or threatens to take that business and relationships across town, to the competitor?

- What about when you try to raise capital to start or grow a business, and you are making your rounds visiting different financial resources, sharing your vision and strategies. Do you want to make sure that these individuals can't make your idea theirs?

Couldn't happen to you?

You might feel like your tiny start-up business is too small to attract legal problems. Not so! A gentleman I know very well decided he wanted to become a partner in a local landscape company. He met with the owner and decided not only to become a partner but to invest a large sum of capital. So the two men drafted a very basic hand-written contract. It wasn't witnessed by anyone. There was only one signed original, and it was kept at the company.

The money was used to buy more equipment and to pay some outstanding payroll obligations. The company continued to operate for nearly a year while the two partners went door-to-door, earning new customers and renewing residual business. After watching the business grow compared to the previous year, my friend began to question why he wasn't earning more from the business's activity. As you can imagine, things got extremely nasty. The original owner finally said something like "Screw you. I don't owe you anything. Don't come around here again."

Then when my friend began asking to see their agreement and financial records about his investment, the original owner said, "I destroyed the contract and I'm not paying you anything. If you don't like it, sue me!" Unfortunately, this eye-opening experience taught my friend some of the hardest lessons of his business life. He spent a year working for next to nothing and lost his entire investment. There *had* been real documentation supporting his claim to owning part of the business—but it was gone. The only recourse he had was to launch a costly legal battle that he probably would have lost. In the end, he wrote off his loss and moved on, but not without a bruised ego and a significantly depleted bank account. Oops.

So what am I saying?

Just remember that starting a small business on a shoe-string budget is not a unique circumstance. I speak for most entrepreneurs. We've all been there. The start-up game involves a lot of difficult decisions, usually choosing among many things, all of which you need. But it's about trying to properly identify what items are the most important related to the stage of the business development process you are currently in.

It is critically important to build a rock-solid foundation for your business. That includes setting up the most appropriate type of entity and business structure, organizing the company to bring on employees and investors, protecting whatever secret sauce you plan on taking to market, and a formidable list of other things. You do need solid legal representation to survive and succeed.

M.O.

The Many Faces of Business Law

*Take a mini-tour of the business law landscape
and see where your company's needs fit in.*

ALMOST ANYTHING AND EVERYTHING you can think of in the legal field
will probably fall under the umbrella of business law in one way or another. It's
one reason many lawyers are drawn to the practice.

For example you might be thinking, "Aha! What about divorce or family
law?" Well, that area is often very relevant in small- and medium-sized businesses,
in terms of their legal representation. Imagine a family business start-up where the
husband and wife both have ownership. If the marital bliss ends, and the couple
divorces, what happens to the business? A cluster of legal issues will need addressing. And that's just one example.

There are many attorneys who specifically identify themselves as business
attorneys. So what do they do? Most likely, they work in a few of the various categories I'll discuss below. To find out, just ask them or research their background.
Do not get confused by titles or advertised practice areas like *corporate* or *business*.
It is more·important to know basically what advice you want. With that defined,
you can decide if a particular attorney is qualified. If you are not sure, just ask the
attorney and check references. If you want to dig deeper, you'll find numerous
industry and jurisdictional-specific books with information and names of attorneys, with checklists or other references on the specifics of what you want to do.

Some of these categories are more common than others and are more
closely associated with a traditional business lawyer, while others are quite specialized. Before we get started, please let my lawyerly mind point out that many,
many books focus on small sections of each of these specialties. This list is not
comprehensive and is only intended to give you an overall view of the range of
topics you will find expertise in.

Agency Law This area addresses relationships, asking who can act on whose behalf. What authority do they have? What responsibilities do they have? Who is ultimately liable for an individual's actions, that individual or the business? What can the individual do on behalf of the business? Who can be an authorized agent?

Alternative Dispute Resolution This area focuses on arbitration, mediation, and negotiation. It asks how we are going to resolve disputes. With customers? (Is the customer always right?) With employees? With suppliers? Disputes will inevitably occur; you must plan for them.

Commercial Code This is called the Uniform Commercial Code in the U.S. Typical issues: How do the commercial codes work in your jurisdiction? What protections are built in for your business that you may use? What is the relation of these codes to your business model?

Commercial Crimes The focus here might be on something your company does (or doesn't do) or something that someone or another company does to you or your company. What things are considered commercial crimes in your jurisdiction? Are they the same in every location in which your business operates? Are there any differences if you cross state lines or ship products internationally? Sometimes what is legal and/or customary in one jurisdiction could be criminal in another. For example, bribes, in many countries, are part of standard business and in others, are a significant crime. On another front, your company could need protection from the criminal acts of employees.

Consumer Protection This specialty asks questions like what rules are related to your interactions with the consumers of your product or service. What liability do you have for your products? What if they break? What if they are used improperly? What are the rules you must follow for contacting your customer to collect a past due bill? Are there specific times of day when you may call? (In the U.S., the answer is *yes*.) Are there required disclosures you have to give? (In the U.S., the answer again is *yes*.) Do you need to have your products tested before they are imported?

Contract Law Contracts, contracts, contracts! They form the core of most businesses' legal needs. They put understandings in writing. You must know what they actually mean. An attorney will help you to protect yourself and ensure you reach your desired results. The goal is to ensure compliance and adherence to the agreement reached. Contracts are very specific, varying by industry and jurisdiction. This is one of the most important areas in which to have an attorney. Every attorney I know updates his or her notes every time a new case is decided or a new issue arises, to ensure that all clients are protected in that situation in the future.

Corporate Law This very broad category includes the formation, modification, documentation, structure, distribution, compliance and control of organizations, just to name a few topics. It's often used as another name for business law.

Employment Law Think human resources here. This area is also broad. Some typical questions include things like these: Should and can you have the employee sign a non-compete agreement? Can you ask the prospective employee about his personal life in a job interview? How often are you required to give an employee a break? When do you have to pay extra for overtime work? If your employee is hurt at work, how does that affect the business? Can an employee sue the business or you for anything? If it has anything to do with employees, then it is probably in this category and there is probably a rule or a case on the subject. Good advice and a little forethought will go a long way to preventing problems here.

Financial Regulation This covers disclosure, taxes, tracking, and reporting, as well as your interactions with local, state and national government agencies. For some industries, your needs can be quite minimal, rarely going beyond standard accounting and tax practices. In other industries, it can be a major portion of your business model.

Intellectual Property This is the world of copyrights, trademarks, patents, business processes, logos, and secret formulas or inventions. The focus is the protection and exploitation of all of these intangible items.

Insolvency This issue could affect your business, but it also can apply to your customers, suppliers and others. Most people believe this is the end of the road (especially those who played too much of the board game of Monopoly as kids). But I encourage you to view solid advice in this area as a powerful, long-term tool you can use. The list of major companies that have faced some form of insolvency, then restructured and went on to become more successful in the long run, is significant and long. Just look at the automobile or airline industries around the world.

Industry-Specific Laws and Regulations In addition to local rules, your industry may have its own very specific rules or regulatory agencies which you need to comply with. Your attorney can help review your particular sector's governance, identify compliance issues, and help you know what to do about them.

International This area of law includes trade regulations, quotas, tariffs and more, not to mention potentially everything else discussed in this whole book, regarding each individual country you trade in. You must consider risks, opportunities and protections provided to your business in foreign countries. In some cases, your local attorney may recommend a counterpart in another country who can facilitate things on that local front much more expertly and economically.

Local Law and Regulation What are the local rules? In the U.S., there can be significant variance from city to city, and county to county, not to mention in multi- or interstate commerce. One of my clients has a tree maintenance firm. His office is located in the unincorporated part of the county (i.e., it's not in a city, so it's subject to county regulations only). The closest city is less than 10 minutes' drive away, yet it requires tree trimmers to carry significantly higher levels of insurance to operate there. Luckily we could discover that for him and protect his business properly. Another client came to see me after he ended up in a bad spot due to an accident that occurred in a certain city. His business was not carrying the required amount of insurance to conduct business there. So this client was potentially facing not only the fallout from the accident, but also personal liability, the revocation of his professional license, and possible civil and criminal fines—all because he did not review the local rules. An attorney can help you determine if there are any local rules that affect your business.

Mergers, Acquisitions, Franchising, Sales and Venture Capital This specialty addresses everything associated with joining a business, acquiring an existing business, franchising or selling your business, and/or financing the startup or growth of your business. These are very specialized areas and vary by industry and size of transaction. You require the aid of an experienced and knowledgeable attorney due to the high risk involved.

Real Estate This includes leases, purchases, sales, and other property transactions. It's one of the most common areas that leads business owners to work with an attorney. Unfortunately, I have met a significant number of clients who initially came in for help because of a commercial lease dispute; upon review it often emerges that the lease is extremely biased against their interests. When asked about it, these business owners say they did not read or review the lease prior to signing, because the landlord told them it was a "standard" lease. Don't make that classic mistake: At least read before you sign, and get help if you question any of the terms.

Taxation This is a very jurisdictionally and industry-specific branch of law. Solid, up-to-date advice can make a significant difference in your business's bottom line and overall success. And don't underestimate the need to heed all warnings and keep excellent records. Far too often, I have seen otherwise successful businesses undone by faulty record keeping and tax audits.

Torts These are intentional wrongs. They can be the acts of individuals acting on behalf of the business or individually, or actions against the business itself. Examples are negligence, product liability, unfair and deceptive trade practices, fraud, misrepresentation, and the like. The aim of legal advice in this area is to provide protection for you and your business and also give you the ability to pursue those who wrong you.

So that's the lay of the land in business law. Here's a practical tip: Make sure that the business attorney you settle on has the specific qualifications and experience needed to provide you with the services you require. For example, I have done a fair amount of business, real estate and financial law throughout my career, but I do not consider myself to be qualified to deal with patent issues or complex commercial litigation that might cross several state or international borders. I would refer any potential client with needs in these areas to an attorney or firm qualified to handle those issues. The client might work with me for matters I'm experienced in and consult a specialist for particular issues outside them.

All in all, if you can develop a list of the kinds of legal advice you are most likely to need, you'll find an individual attorney or a legal firm that can cover most of them and which can link you up with any specialized expertise you need that they cannot supply themselves. Armed with such advisors, you can avoid lots of problems and concentrate on building your business.

M.R.M.

Business Models for
Your Legal Representation

*Before you set up meetings with potential legal
representatives, get the low-down on various
business models for paying for their advice.*

A CORPORATE LAWYER usually does a mix of some of the things you just read about in the section above. While every business has its own unique ways of managing legal counsel, the financial side of this relationship usually falls into predictable business models. If you are in the early days of a one-person start-up, your needs might be rather simple, but it will be good for you to get a feel for the complete picture anyway. The initial distinction you must consider is whether the lawyer is in-house counsel or outside counsel.

In-house or outside?

In-house counsel is often referred to as **corporate counsel**, and a company with this arrangement is usually fairly sizeable or has significant revenues. These attorneys generally work full time, as direct employees of the business they serve. They will not have an outside practice or be a member of any outside law firms. The in-house counsel can be a single attorney, or a group of attorneys and perhaps support staff. Their primary job is to advise the executive level management team regarding the legal implications of major strategic decisions. Based on the business structure, they may also serve as the business's legal department, handling other daily business tasks like collections, contracts or negotiations.

Attorneys who work as corporate counsel are often known as jacks of many trades because they spend most of their time researching, evaluating and advising, not litigating in court. The corporate counsel will bring in outside counsel with specialized experience to assist in complex or unique legal matters. Most states in the U.S. make exceptions in their bar rules related to corporate counsel, specifically that they may not have to take the bar examination for every state that their business operates in. It is very common for corporate counsel attorneys to move into business leadership positions rather than back into traditional legal practice; hence a fair proportion of CEOs are also attorneys.

Outside counsel are attorneys or law firms in private practice who practice in corporate or business law, or specialize in a related niche. They generally work full time for themselves or a law firm. Your business will be one of a number of clients that the outside counsel may have. One advantage of working with outside counsel is that you are free to work with as many attorneys as you choose. For example, a business might employ one attorney for collection matters, another attorney for real estate transactions and a firm for intellectual property matters. Outside counsel spend the majority of their time working on specific issues. Their representation will be limited to those issues, and they will have little to no involvement in business operations or decision making.

As we've seen, attorneys who work in private practice often specialize in a limited number of practice areas. They focus on continuing education in those specific areas and build a reputation for excellence in them. They often decline cases that are not directly related to their areas of expertise. Outside counsel must be specifically licensed, qualified and admitted to each court they appear in; thus their representation may not easily cross jurisdictional boundaries. Some attorneys do move from private practice to the role of corporate counsel, but it is more common for them to remain in private practice and build either their firm or personal book of business.

Cost considerations

Every business is unique. As an entrepreneur it will be an important business decision for you, when you decide what type of counsel to employ (or work with), and at what point to consider hiring in-house counsel.

This move is not usually part of a small business model. However, there is a growing trend in medium-size businesses to hire an in-house attorney, as the costs of hiring less experienced attorneys has decreased significantly in the past ten years. Many medium-sized businesses are identifying ways to utilize an attorney on staff to significantly increase profitability. For example, a medium-size car dealership hired its own in-house attorney. They realized a significant increase in profits by having the attorney handle all collection matters as well as reviewing and executing the sales contracts with clients, among other duties.

Hiring counsel and retainer models

If you are hiring in-house counsel, then the process will look just like hiring any employee of the business. If you are hiring outside counsel, you will have three basic hiring options:

- For a specific time period—called a true retainer

- For a specific issue

- For ongoing representation

Each attorney will have her own representation options, billing and contracts. (Yes, you will absolutely be required to sign a contract. It's a habit you must get into for all transactions.) You must discuss this with your attorney.

First, let's look at the **true retainer model**, where you retain an attorney for a specific time period. You pay the attorney an agreed fee, and in exchange the attorney will ensure that he is available to handle any legal matters for your business that arise. Also, he will not take any cases against your business for that specific time period. Other than the initial "true retainer" fee, there may not be any additional charges for the entire period. Some view it as almost legal insurance.

Second, you can consider **retaining an attorney for a specific issue or individual case**, hiring the attorney to represent you in a single matter through the completion of that matter, regardless how long it takes. This is the most common type of legal representation and is what most people think of when they hire an attorney. Typical issues might be buying some land or equipment, preparing a patent application, or hiring (or firing) a high-profile employee.

Finally, there is **retaining for ongoing representation.** This generally requires a significant retainer fee. But you can contact and use the services of the attorney as needed on multiple legal issues. The simplicity of this arrangement makes it a very common method for getting legal representation. It's also flexible: In one month you may require services such as having a contract reviewed, drafting demand letters, and researching the applicable laws for a new project. The next month you may not require any services at all. Obviously both you and the attorney will want to review the work flow vs. compensation balance from time to time and adjust as your needs require.

Billing methods

Private practice attorneys generally charge for their services using one of three billing methods: flat fee service, hourly billing, or a contingency fee agreement.

Flat fee services are most common in simple matters where the expectations on both sides are very clear and there is little chance of deviation from the service to be provided. Examples would include the review of simple documents, drafting of simple documents, or appearing at unopposed legal proceedings.

Hourly billing is the most common type of billing for private practice attorneys. Most states in the U.S. require the attorney provide in writing the hourly rates for anyone who could bill on your matter. This could include the attorney, partners, associates, paralegals, legal assistants or other staff. You can then verify whether these rates are in accordance with the market rates.

Finally, **contingency billing** is where the attorney only gets paid if you recover what you feel is due you. This method is used only in specific practice areas like personal injury or medical malpractice.

Hourly billing issues

While hourly billing terrifies most clients initially, it is very important to understand that it is by far the best way to buy legal services, especially in business law or when there are unknowns in the matter.

Here's why. You, the client, expect a certain level of service and full diligence given to your affairs. If you have agreed to pay a fixed amount and you feel it is unreasonably high for the service you receive, it is unlikely you will continue to retain the attorney at that rate for very long. If the fixed amount you pay is either fair or too low, then the attorney has a financial incentive to complete work on your matters by doing the least work possible. (More money and less work means higher profitability for the attorney. Higher profitability is good. Remember, your attorney is a for-profit business too).

In contrast, with hourly billing, you are only billed for work actually done. You can request more or less attention to be given to your various matters. And your attorney knows that she will be accurately compensated for all work she actually does for you.

Yes, yours is a small start-up and you watch costs like a hawk. And everyone knows someone who has a horror story related to hourly billing. But that can be mitigated in multiple ways:

- Periodic account statements. Every law office and state bar has policies, rules and rates related to statements. You have the right to receive, review, and if need be, question them on a regular basis, just like you do with all other business expenses.

- Selecting the right attorney for your needs. As with any other area of your business, you should research, evaluate and then select a quality attorney. This may include getting referrals and reviews and tapping your own intuition. Most attorneys are building their own practices, which are of course businesses, so their reputations and long-term relationships are important considerations for their financial success as well.

- Clear communication. Billing should be transparent. If an issue arises, it should be dealt with immediately. You and your attorney are a team, working towards the success of your business. Your attorney can be one of your greatest resources, and you must ensure that neither billing nor communication problems impair that cohesive relationship.

Attorneys often have minimum retainer balances. If your account balance falls below the minimum, you may be required to make a payment to get the balance back up to the minimum requirement. They may also have a minimum monthly billing or administrative cost, especially with long-term clients. Law firms are one of the most heavily regulated professions, especially the financial accounting of client funds. Thus, most law firms will have fixed costs associated with an active client and account. These firms will offset these costs with monthly minimum billings, i.e., a mandatory monthly case review by an attorney, or a monthly administrative maintenance fee. Each law firm will also have its own policy for costs such as copies, postage or filing fees, which may be a separate cost retainer or monthly cost invoicing. Make sure you are clear on the total billing and methods used so that you can accurately budget for legal expenses.

A corporate lawyer represents the interests of your business to the rest of the world. You have many options for obtaining the legal representation you need, as well as options for paying for your attorney's services. Since your corporate lawyer can be one of your greatest business assets, invest all the time and effort you need to pick the one who will best fit your needs.

M.R.M.

How Do I Find the Right Attorney for My Needs?

Go with the first listing in the phone book. (Ha-ha!)

IF YOU WANT TO FIND a good outside corporate attorney for your new or prospective business, you can start by asking friends, family and trusted colleagues for candidates with stand-up reputations in your community or industry. Everybody has one or more contacts who can point you toward legal resources they know about or have worked with themselves.

Then you'll need to make sure the candidates you've discovered have the particular expertise and topical focus that match your business's needs. You can do some of this online, or by making use of referral services you might find in small business advisory agencies, the local bar association, business management consultants, chambers of commerce, trade associations, and the like.

It's also important to think about your budget and your timetable. Some attorneys will be able to start working with you immediately, while others have projects and client needs slotted ahead of you.

There are other important considerations:

- Quality vs. cost
- Accessibility of the attorney
- Experience of the attorney and firm
- Long-term nature of the relationship
- Ability to take new clients
- Needs of your business
- Social or personal nature of the relationship

Let's suppose that you come up with several candidates. Now what? What things should you look out for? Here are some preliminary questions, assuming you are meeting with a senior attorney in a firm. You can adjust them appropriately if you are considering a single, independent attorney:

- Who will be doing the majority of the work?

- If there is research to be done, will that be handled by a paralegal?

- If yes, what is the rate for your paralegals?

- If not, what is the hourly rate for an associate attorney?

- What is the hourly rate for your time?

- Do you offer flat rates? If not, how many hours will this project take?

- If you are discussing a particular project, ask how much various activities within the project will cost.

Your initial, exploratory consultation may be free of charge, though some higher profile firms do charge for one. However, many of them will credit that amount if you commit to using them as a resource moving forward.

Often the most respected member of a firm (a senior partner or a name-on-the-door type) will introduce you to the firm and its services. This attorney is often not the person who will be handling your needs once you sign a service agreement. More than once, early in my career, I contracted with legal resources for different projects and later found out that a paralegal did most of the preliminary research and document prep. Sometimes the document prep would be original and other times it would start as a template that the firm had in archive. And there have been instances where I thought the quick-witted attorney with the expensive designer suit and her name on the building was going to be handling my contract negotiations. But in fact, a junior or associate attorney who passed the bar exam the Friday before was going to be drafting a letter on my behalf and sending it over to the other party's firm for review. This made me feel (and perhaps look) like an idiot.

Delegation occurs in a law firm the way it does in every business. If you want a specific partner or attorney, then you need to communicate that and be prepared pay for the services requested. Experienced senior attorneys in this area of practice often charge triple or more what an associate with less than five year's experience would charge.

Also, as part of the way attorneys are regulated, managing partners of law firms are fully liable for the actions and practice of all associates, so it is extremely rare that an unqualified attorney would be allowed to handle a case unsupervised.

These cautions are not meant to slam paralegals or junior associates. Paralegals are specialists whose work allows law firms to leverage their senior members' time, and they can save you lots of money as well as speed up the work on your matters. Likewise, younger attorneys can bring energy, creativity, technical savvy and other qualities to their work that can offset what they may lack in experience. The point here is that you must clearly understand who's doing what and what it will cost, and you should feel comfortable asking for the most appropriate people to perform certain tasks.

As with so many things in business, this is where "Buyer Beware" is good advice. Be cautious when you find firms that are willing to engage in projects at a fraction of the cost of others. Confirm that appropriate personnel are handling the items you want them to handle and have it spelled out in your service contract. A blanket contract appointing XYZ Law Firm to handle your needs is not sufficient.

Don't be afraid to probe candidates

It's completely normal for a business to interview a number of legal resources to find the firm or individual that most closely matches its needs based on size, scale, expertise and business style. Attorneys and law firms come in all different shapes and sizes. There is an appropriate resource out there for every business's needs. So evaluate costs, location, proposed strategies, and how much they are focused on billings vs. going beyond expectations to show their commitment to the relationship. Really get a feel for who they are and what they are about.

Frankly, if you are a small business owner, you probably don't need a high-profile firm representing your interests. Often you can find the same quality of work in smaller firms that specialize in working with individuals and businesses of your size. Whatever you do, don't just call the firm with the most public advertising or the full-page ad in the phone book or online. Their marketing budget is not necessarily a reflection of their skillset. These resources could be great, but I've noticed that they seem to charge higher hourly rates. It might just have something to do with paying for all that marketing and promotion.

M.O.

What Does a Corporate Lawyer Do?

It's called taking care of (your) business.

NOW THAT YOU KNOW your options for getting legal representation, the types of specialization you can tap within corporate law, the business models available for paying for your attorney's services, and how to locate and pick a good match for your business needs, we can ask and answer a fundamental question: What does a corporate lawyer actually *do*?

Answer: represent your business entity to the outside world. It seems like a very simple answer. But there is some extremely important lawyerly fine print related to that answer, so please read on very carefully.

At some point in your start-up phase, you will most likely turn your proposed business into some type of business entity (see more on this on pages 43-44). The majority of these possible business organizations are actually independent entities, each with its own tax ID number, bank account, liability, legal requirements, etc. Essentially, a business entity is just that: an independent non-human entity, a straw person, a pseudo-individual, even a humanoid. Call it by whatever name that helps you picture that the entity now has a separate life with rights and obligations distinct and separate from those of its owners, shareholders, partners, members, etc.

Your corporate lawyer *represents the interests of the business entity,* **not** *necessarily the individuals associated with the business.* (That's the absolutely important fine print.) The business could potentially have interests that are different from or even opposed to the interests of individuals associated with the business, such as the founder, a partner, a shareholder or member.

These situations, where interests diverge, are far more common than you might expect. The business's interests are determined based on the type of organization and decision-making process it has, as declared in the formation and administration documents of the business. The most common examples of divergence are hostile takeovers (when a new faction gains a controlling percentage of voting shares and replaces the corporate leadership or liquidates the company), the execution of corporate estate planning (when a partner in a business dies and her ownership transfers to other partners and not to her estate), or the realignment of voting blocks in a closely held company.

Here's a real-life example of the last situation. I was involved in a case in which three brothers founded a very successful business. Abe was the one that made it all happen and ran the daily operations as CEO. Bert worked there on a daily basis and essentially did the research and menial tasks. Charlie was part of the company in name only. The brothers structured the company by distributing the ownership shares as follows:

Abe got 40 percent, while Bert and Charlie each got 30 percent.

Well, at one point, Abe and Bert had a falling out. Abe, acting as CEO, hired a law firm to sue Bert on behalf of the business, for some alleged wrong. However, Charlie sided with Bert. They got together and, using their 60 percent majority, appointed a new CEO. On behalf of the business entity, the new CEO then directed the law firm to drop the suit against Bert, and then asked the firm to proceed with a suit against Abe! The law firm had to follow the instructions of *its client, the business.*

The lesson here is that you may have founded your company, or you may be a major figure in it. But you are not the business, no matter how much you identify with it, and your company's legal representative is not your personal watchdog—she's the company's face to the world.

M.R.M.

CHAPTER II

Start-Up Activities

Choosing the Right Business Entity

*When conceptualizing a new venture, entrepreneurs must
consider which type of business entity will suit
it best. Start your business the right
way by addressing this first.*

YOU PAY BILLS EVERY month to businesses like Jack's Garage, Tax Prep LLC, and Green Utility Corporation. Each of these businesses has a unique corporate structure. When you set up yours, you need to pick the best type of business structure to suit your great idea.*

Whether you set up your business as a sole proprietorship, partnership, limited liability company (LLC), S-Corporation, or C-Corporation, it is vital to understand not only the filing and paperwork requirements, but also the different tax implications and liability impacts that each choice entails.

Sole proprietorships: Commonly, owner-operated small businesses are set up as sole proprietorships due to the simplicity of the filings and regulation, as well as the single-layer tax impact on the revenues of the business. This type of ownership also allows you, the owner, to be your own boss. However, you should be extremely cautious if you set up either as a sole proprietor or in a general partnership. Both types of business structures allow for all of the liabilities of the business to be shared with the individual owners on a personal level. Unlimited liability can be scary. Just remember to hope for the best but plan for the worst. Don't choose a business structure based on the ease and convenience of setting it up.

It is more common than one would think to have business situations end in lawsuits resulting in general partners and sole proprietors being sued personally and losing homes, cars and savings accounts. There are plenty of hurdles that

*While the examples and names of types of businesses in this section are from the United States, the general structure of businesses is much the same worldwide. This section and the two following it first appeared in our book, *Starting a Business* (Nova Vista Publishing, ISBN 978-90-77256-36-7).

these types of business owners have to overcome. Management can be difficult with limited participants and there is commonly an overwhelming time commitment associated with this type of business.

Partnerships: There are two types of members in a partnership—a general partner and a limited partner. General partners have unlimited liability and are typically managers of the company. Limited partners have exactly what you would think—limited liability, and they usually do not have a role managing the company. Just remember, no matter how well the individual partners get along, one of the most common issues with partnerships is the disagreements that arise among members. This sometimes leads to unfortunate fallings-out among friends.

Corporations: Most successful types of businesses are corporations—either limited liability companies (LLCs) or conventional corporations (C-Corporations). They generate approximately 80 percent of all sales in the United States and they all share two major benefits. First, they have limited liability, and second, they usually qualify for special tax advantages that other types of business ownerships do not enjoy. (An S-Corporation is actually not a business entity; it's a tax election or choice that causes all income to be passed through to the owners, thereby eliminating the double taxation of traditional corporations. More on that in a moment.)

Incorporating a business is a great strategy. It allows for the company to grow, it has perpetual life, makes change of ownership easy, and it's common for corporations to be able to afford talented employees. However, there are some disadvantages to incorporating a business. Corporations cost more to start than sole proprietorships or partnerships, they require more paperwork, and conflicts among owners and board members can arise. They are also affected by double taxation, which means that the business's profits will be taxed, as well as the shareholders' dividends.

Let's revisit the S-Corp for a moment. It's a tax election, not an entity per se. It offers single taxation, like in a partnership. Downsides of incorporating as an S-Corporation include ineligibility for a dividends-received deduction, and S-Corps are not subject to the 10 percent of taxable income limitation that is applicable to charitable contribution deductions.

A limited liability company (LLC) is a form of business in which owners and managers receive the limited liability and tax benefits of an S-Corporation without having to conform to the S-Corporation restrictions. For certain professions, e.g., accounting, architecture, and medical or psychological care, the LLC becomes a PLLC, a professional limited liability company.

Choosing the best type of business is a personal choice, and it's certainly one that shouldn't be taken lightly. This is an area where professional advice, tailored to your locality and business sector, is essential. Seriously analyze your business's projected longevity, growth and future development before making your choice.

S.G. and M.R.M.

The Difference Between Copyrights and Trademarks

*Ensure that you're protecting your intellectual
property the right way.*

BLACKSMITHS WHO MADE swords in the Roman Empire may have been the first trademark users. In later times, copyright law applied only to the copying of books. Patents are recorded as early as 500 BC among the Greeks, giving people who invented new recipes one year's exclusive use of the dish.

Protection of your intellectual property (IP) should be your very first step when starting a new business or project that depends on your IP. Also, just because you've conjured up a great concept or idea doesn't mean that you're the first to come up with it. Do yourself a favor before you start marketing your new idea and check with the appropriate government offices in order to ensure that you're not accidentally taking credit for something someone else has already registered or copyrighted.

Below is a list of Fun Facts that you may not have known about copyright and trademarking. These similar, but legally different, protection practices cover different things. By all means, seek legal advice if you have any questions on these subjects.

A copyright is a set of exclusive rights granted by a state to the creator of an original work (or the creator's assignee) for a limited period of time, upon disclosure of the work. This includes the right to copy, distribute and adapt the work.

A trademark is a distinctive sign or indicator used by an individual, business organization, or other legal entity, used to identify that the products or services to consumers with which the trademark appears originate from a unique source, and to distinguish its products or services from those of other entities.

A copyright protects works of authorship as fixed in a tangible form of expression. Examples of what a copyright covers include works of art, photos, pictures, graphic designs, drawings, songs, music and sound recordings of all kinds, books, manuscripts, publications and other written works, plays, software, movies, shows, and other performance arts. If you are interested in protecting a title, slogan, or other short word phrase, then generally, you want a trademark.

© is the copyright symbol in a copyright notice

™ is the symbol for an unregistered trademark (a mark to promote a brand or goods)

ˢᴹ is the symbol for an unregistered service mark (a mark to promote or brand services)

® is the symbol for a registered trademark and a registered service mark

In the U.S., copyright is obtained through the United States Copyright Office (USCO), which is a division of the Library of Congress (see www.copyright.gov). Other countries have similar offices, which you can locate on the web.

Likewise, in the U.S., trademark is obtained through the United States Patent and Trademark Office (USPTO, at www.uspto.gov). Check the web for other countries' offices.

Keep in mind that there may be occasions when both copyright and trademark protection are desirable for the same project. For example, a marketing campaign for a new product may introduce a new slogan for use with the product, which also appears in advertisements for the product. The advertisement's text and graphics, as published, are covered by copyright. That will not, however, protect the slogan in your ad. The slogan may be protected by trademark law, but that law will not cover the rest of the advertisement. If you want both forms of protection, you will have to perform both types of registration with the appropriate offices.

The websites of the respective offices of control in countries around the world offer a wealth of further information, ranging from tutorials and step-by-step walk-throughs to other valuable information that can get you on your way to protecting your intellectual property. Don't neglect to do so.

S.G.

How to Patent a New Product

A step-by-step guide to getting your product patented.

ALL TOO OFTEN, we hear about peoples' dreams of starting a business being bogged down by government paperwork. They complain that because of it, their great plans to start a new business based on a product or invention they have developed never get off the ground. The patenting process seems too overwhelming to them.

Take Europe, for example. Presently, although there exists a mechanism through the European Patent Office (EPO) for challenging and verifying a granted patent's validity, the process is limited to a nine-month period of opposition, beginning the day the patent is granted. Beyond that, a centralized way of challenging a patent granted by the EPO does not exist. Contracting states of the EPO must each separately validate a granted patent. It then becomes the responsibility of each contracting state to enforce and challenge the granted rights. It's truly a bureaucratic maze. (More information for obtaining a patent in Europe can be found at www.epo.org.)

For entrepreneurs in Australia, the patent process is very similar to that of the U.S. The patenting process in Australia begins at www.ipaustralia.gov.au and roughly follows the same steps as the U.S. procedure.

Here is a step-by-step guide, with the U.S. procedures serving as an example, to getting past the patent paperwork and on your way to building your new business.

1. First, you need to find out if your product has already been patented. You can accomplish this by running a simple search with the United States Patent and Trademark Office (USPTO) on their website, www.uspto.gov. If you discover that someone has already patented your idea, then sorry: Unless you think of a new way to use your product, there isn't much you can do.

2. If your product hasn't already been patented, your next step is to decide what type of patent you want to apply for. There are three types: (1) Design Patents (for ornamental characteristics), (2) Plant Patents (for new varieties of asexually produced plants), or the most common (3) Utility Patents (for useful processes, machines, articles of manufacture, or the composition of matter).

3. Once you decide which of the three types of patents fits your idea best, you must determine a filing strategy. Decide whether you want to file in the U.S. only, or if you want International Protection. International Protection involves international cooperation among various worldwide Intellectual Property Offices. If you foresee international business, it's best to go with International Protection.

4. Assuming that you want to file a Utility Patent, which is the most common type, you will next need to decide if you want to file a Provisional or Non-Provisional Application. Don't be scared by the long words. Basically, Provisional filings are informal and rather quick, while Non-Provisional filings are formal and involve a much more tedious process. While the Provisional process is easier, we recommend taking the time and effort, if possible, to protect your idea more fully by completing the Non-Provisional Application process.

5. The fifth step is optional. It is expedited examination. The USPTO offers an Accelerated Examination Program whereby, basically, if you meet certain qualifications, you can "jump the line" and get your patent processed faster.

6. Now you're ready to make the final decision before filing: Who will actually do it? Will you file yourself (which is called *pro se*) or use a registered attorney or agent? While many people undertake the process of filing themselves, we recommend that you use an attorney or agent to complete the actual filing. This will ensure that your application is not returned or delayed for inadequate completion. This is a perfect example of having to spend a little money to make money, but it's definitely worth it in the long run.

7. Next, you or your attorney or agent gather needed elements for electronic filing. Here, you determine your application processing fees and apply for a customer number and digital certificate. You can do all this directly on the USPTO website. Your customer number allows you to easily manage all of your filings and correspondence with the USPTO and your digital certificate is a security measure that will uniquely iden-

tify you and allow you secure access to your patent information and data.

8.   Now it's time to actually apply for your patent. In the U.S., we recommend that you use the USPTO's Electronic Filing System (EFS) as a registered eFiler. Using the EFS, anyone with an Internet connection can file patent applications and documents without downloading special software or changing document preparation tools and processes.

9.   The good news about the ninth step is that you don't have to do anything! After you (or your attorney or agent) have completed the eighth step and submitted your application, the ninth step involves the USPTO's examination of your application. You can check your application status at any point on the website, using your Customer Number and Digital Certificate from Step 7. At the end of this step, if the USPTO gives you a "thumbs up" and your application is accepted, congratulations! Jump down to Step 12!

10.   If the USPTO doesn't accept your application on the first try, it's no big deal. Don't get discouraged. You have several options here. You can file replies, requests for reconsideration, and appeals as necessary.

11.   This step is another one in which you need not take any action. Step 11 is the USPTO's reply to your request or appeal from Step 10. If, after your appeal or request, the USPTO decides to overturn their rejection and accepts your application, they will send you a Notice of Allowance and charge you for any fees that you may owe from their additional attention.

12.   The good news, if you've made it to this point in the patent filing process, is that your patent has been accepted and only one small step stands in your way before your patent is granted! The bad news is that now, you have to pay the issuing and publication fees. Once the USPTO processes your payment, the patent is granted and your product is protected.

13.   One final step involves the preservation of your protection. Maintenance fees are due at 3.5, 7.5, and 11.5 years after the initial patent is granted.

It must be said that the United States Patent and Trademark Office has done an exceptional job streamlining their electronic filing and informational system. In the U.S., patenting through the USPTO is the only recognized option, but they make it easy and affordable. To learn more, see their website at www.uspto.gov.

S.G.

Renting and Leasing Property for Your Business

Your business may be brick and mortar or virtual, but you still need some kind of space in which to work.

THE MOST COMMON TRANSACTIONS regarding real estate deal with renting and leasing. However, there are many other situations that blend business interests, law and real estate. Are you thinking about leasing an office space or retail storefront? Subleasing extra space to another business? Are you a tenant in a strip shopping center or mall where an anchor tenant has moved out? Is your city considering changing the direction of traffic flow, the parking laws or the name of the street where your shop is? These issues are vitally important to your business's success. We will get back to some of them later in this section.

Since most start-ups work on tight budgets, we won't focus on buying property for your business here. If you need to purchase land or space right away, work with a real estate attorney, but read this section to acquaint yourself with some issues you'll need to consider anyway. If you are among the many entrepreneurs who start out by renting or leasing space, let's look now at some basic concepts that you will find in most landlord/tenant negotiations.

A lease is a written contract that sets up terms under which the Lessor (the owner or landlord, who can be a person or a company) and Lessee or Tenant (you) agree to let you use the owner's property (land, building, equipment) for a defined, fairly long period of time under defined terms, which could be variable or adjustable. Those terms stay in effect for the entire term (life) of the contract. The benefit to both the Lessor and Lessee of a lease is its fixed, stable nature. If a lease feels too tightly binding for your new business in its early days, by all means consider renting, but be aware that the landlord can change terms, raise rents, evict you and so forth, short-term. However, you can also move on short notice!

So not surprisingly, small businesses with simple property needs sometimes start by renting and then change to leasing once the business picture seems stable.

Commercial property leases

The first step is to understand a commercial lease, i.e., what you will be negotiating and agreeing to when leasing space. It is important to fully understand the different elements of a commercial lease and how it differs from a basic residential lease agreement. Keep in mind that you can always elect to work with a real estate professional that specializes in tenant representation for commercial real estate deals. These trained professionals known what to look for and what to avoid.

The next step is to clearly identify what you need: how much space, what location, the type of space, budget, build-out assistance or tenant allowance, signage, deferred rent, CAM (Common Area Maintenance) etc. Again, if you don't feel comfortable determining these variables then you may want a professional to advise on pros and cons and to represent your interests.

Once you find a suitable property, you can ask the landlord for a draft of the lease. This document should outline the terms and conditions of your proposed lease agreement. It should be as specific as possible, including all necessary detail on these things, plus any special considerations you may need:

- The space in question

- The actual term of the lease in months or years

- The different ways the rent will be calculated

- Proposals for fees for space and other items

- Revenue thresholds that must be met in order for the lease to continue to exist

- Expected move-in dates

- The condition of the property at move-in time

- Percentage of revenue due the owner, if applicable

- Common Area Maintenance (CAM), if applicable

- How taxes will be addressed

- Any other costs associated with the potential lease agreement

Common types of leases

Leases come in several varieties, and can be customized as needed. Skim through the following discussion and then give some thought to what suits your business best.

Gross or Full-Service Lease This is the most basic and least common business lease; it includes everything. The agreed-upon lease fee covers the cost of the space but also insurance, tax, maintenance, utilities, trash, etc. It's the most straightforward type of lease, and it's easy understand the total costs and commitments involved. It will have escalation clauses to protect landlords from rising cost in maintenance, insurance and taxes. These clauses often use a prior year or current year's total expense load as what is called a *base year*. These financials are used to set the *base* for expected expenses that will be incurred once your lease begins. Typically the lease payments include the lease fee and expense load referenced in the base year, but any additional expenses or increases in expense will be incurred by you, factored proportionally by how many square feet or meters of space you occupy.

Net Lease This type of lease can have a variable structure. It is commonly used in environments with mostly industrial tenants, where you find variability in their usage of things like utilities. In this type of lease, you are directly responsible for everything outside of the agreed-upon lease fee. So you will pay for the space, and then pay separately for insurance, maintenance, cleaning, taxes, utilities, etc.

Modified or Hybrid Lease These leases are common, and usually are a hybrid between a net and a gross lease. Often a tenant will pay for the space, insurance and proportional taxes, but there will be some kind of negotiated arrangement for how maintenance and other expenses will be handled.

Common lease terms, clauses and provisions

You will run into various technical terms in rental agreements. Each one needs careful consideration, as it can affect your bottom line or cause future problems if you don't think long term.

Escalation Clause This very basic clause, found in full-service leases, protects the landlord from rising costs associated with taxes, insurance, maintenance, etc. The calculations commonly used for the escalation clause impacts are *base year* and *expense stop* (see those items below).

Use Clause A clause used by landlords to either specify what the use of the space and the operation of your business can be, or to specify what you can't do with the space. They are nightmares, due to the unforeseeable changes that businesses and their products go through as they evolve. Try to avoid these at all costs.

Exclusive Clause Similar to the Use Clause. Have you ever wondered why there is rarely a bakery or a deli in the same strip shopping center as a full-service grocery store? It's because of this clause. Often larger, more powerful tenants will ask for exclusive rights to market or sell certain products or services for an entire property. This limits competition from neighboring business in the same development. If you're the big fish, it's good.

Restrictive Use Clause This is the reciprocal of an exclusive clause, and it affects you if you are the small fish. If you are moving into an already established development with other tenants, you many find a restrictive clause. This clause will outline the items, services and business practices that you are prohibited from engaging in while in the space.

Permissive Use Clause Similar to a use clause, in that the language of the clause outlines what you *can* do in the space. Often these clauses are produced after a prospective tenant lists the activities that she plans on doing. Therefore just make sure to list *everything*, and I mean *everything*, that you many want to do in the space—now, next month, next year, or even five years down the road.

Expense Stop This is the alternative to using a Base Year calculation. When an agreement is being drafted, often a landlord will simply set a expense number (the expense stop). It is the prospective tenant's responsibility to make sure the amount makes sense. Once the expense stop is agreed on, then any expenses that exceed this amount, either monthly, yearly, etc. depending on how the agreement is written, will be yours to pay.

Base Year As mentioned above in the Gross Lease discussion, a base year is the total expenses incurred in a year, usually the current year or prior year, that is used as a base amount in a new lease agreement. Future expense must not exceed that amount, or the increase in expense will be passed on to you.

Common Area Maintenance (CAM) This is an additional charge you must pay for things like window cleaning, elevator (lift) maintenance, and so forth—things that benefit the whole property's function. It's based on the proportion of the space you occupy. Unfortunately it can be a fairly large number relative to the agreed-upon rent amount, so be careful. Your monthly CAM contribution can be 20 percent of your rent or more.

Percentage of Sales This common provision requires you to pay a percentage of revenue to the landlord. It's common in shopping malls and retail spaces and usually doesn't kick in until your business volume reaches a certain revenue threshold.

Some typical scenarios

Now that you've become an expert on commercial real estate, let's get back to those head-spinning scenarios we considered at the start of this section.

What if an anchor tenant moves out of the shopping center? Happily, most retail leases are outfitted with a clause that triggers a significant reduction in rent or even releases you from the lease agreement, allowing you to move out if an anchor tenant moves out. Before you sign a proposed agreement, make sure such events are addressed in an acceptable way.

What happens if I can't make a lease payment? The best thing you can do in this situation is to be honest with your landlord and see if you can work something out, depending on whether your constraints are temporary or permanent. If they are permanent, it's not the end of the world, but you may have to get permission from the landlord and/or work with her to sublet or find another tenant for your space.

What if a unit of government changes the rules affecting my leased property? Sometimes the bigger picture changes and your leased property is affected by things such as changed zoning ordinances, new parking and street plans, energy farms being planted, and so forth. It pays to keep your ears open for pre-implementation hearings and public discussions about these things, as that's your opportunity to protest or try to modify plans that negatively impact you. Ideally, you, your landlord and fellow tenants will be on the same side of the issue. But regardless of your positions, you may want to bring in your attorney to represent you in public discussions. She can research the current rules and the context of the proposed changes and might be able to argue more persuasively (on paper or live) than you about your concerns.

We can't possibly cover every scenario and situation that may arise when dealing with commercial real estate and negotiations. But these basics should shed some very valuable light into the world of tenant/landlord business dealings, and start you thinking about what to look for and what to avoid. Armed with your conclusions, and if necessary, a good real estate attorney, you can deal with issues and then re-focus your attention on what goes on in the space you occupy.

M.R.M.

Everybody Wants a Piece of You: Licenses, Regulations and Taxes

Don't worry, I have a license to do that...

THE TYPICAL ENTREPRENEUR starts a business with a head full of dreams and plans and a huge store of energy to accomplish them. For some, the glowing visions are cramped by the demands of government, their professional organizations, and tax authorities. While you may find these impositions annoying, in most cases it's a waste of your precious energy to fight or evade regulation. Plan for the requirements that apply to you and your business and move on to the goals that fired you up in the first place.

Licenses

Business or professional licenses are permits issued by government agencies or professional regulatory organizations that allow businesses or individuals to operate a business or practice a profession within a certain jurisdiction.

Getting a license usually requires three basic steps: application, registration and qualification.

- Application is the formal process of requesting the license. It can be as simple as a one-page form or could include requirements like affidavits in support, proof of financial assets or completion of prerequisites, etc. Each application is unique and should be reviewed and completed carefully.

- Registration is the ongoing requirement to notify the regulating agency of ongoing business information. This includes information like your current business addresses, the basic financial status of the business, and continued evidence of complying with all business requirements, like having insurance or a medical doctor on staff.

- Qualification is the process of meeting all initial requirements to attain a particular license. This may only be a business address within the county and a small fee, or it could be a full background check and written examinations.

The various types of licenses

Professional service licenses include doctors, lawyers, teachers, tradespeople, and service industry workers. These are individuals regulated by a governmental agency. Most will require continuing education in their profession and other ongoing professional standards, such as ethical and lawful behavior, in order to maintain the quality of the profession. Each profession will have individualized requirements for licensure, education and professional standards.

Professional business licenses include the businesses associated with the abovementioned regulated professions, such as medical clinics, law firms, schools, skilled labor enterprises and restaurants. These are business organizations regulated by a governmental agency. Most will require ongoing certification of compliance with professional standards of care related to business operation and participation by qualified professionals in the operation of the business.

Business licenses for specific industries in which the business is regulated and licensed beyond the individual members of the business. Examples include construction, cosmetology, farm labor, real estate, hotels, restaurants, cooperatives, chemicals, gambling, etc. The business must acquire licensure and meet operational standards, be subject to inspection, and meet other industry-specific requirements. Depending on the industry, there may be individual requirements related to employees for the business to maintain its license. For example, a timeshare property might have to have a qualified manager appointed through the state, a yacht broker could be required to maintain a surety bond or letter of credit, and many sectors must comply with periodic reporting requirements.

Geographic location licenses are licenses to operate a business in a particular geographic location, e.g., a city, county, region, state or country. These entities may require multiple and overlapping licenses. And a business with multiple locations could require multiple licenses for each unit. You will need to verify that the zoning for your location is appropriate for your business. This can be an important issue for some home-based businesses.

Specific action or risk licenses are licenses related to very specific actions, such as illuminated signage, display of giant inflatable balloons, dancing gorillas out front or extreme noise for a set period (e.g., a concert, contest or event). Licenses can be required for routine actions like the preparation or sale of certain foods that could require additional permits from the health department. These can also be associated with particular risks like fire, pollution or hazardous chemicals.

Sales and tax licenses are related to the sale or resale of goods. This is critical to verify, especially if you are conducting sales through the Internet and across multiple jurisdictions. There are significant differences between jurisdictions. Failure to pay or plan for proper taxes could lead to significant financial, civil and possibly even criminal consequences, not to mention sinking your business.

What do I do?

It can be bewildering to face these things, but that's the nature of the game. If you are just starting up, this might be a good time to see if your local business community offers help for starters, specifically in this area. Talk to contacts in your sector, but be wary of their information until you verify it yourself for your own business.

However you do it, find out who regulates your business. Expect that it could be multiple entities, such as national, state and county governmental agencies. You could also be regulated by industry-specific agencies such as the Bar Association or a certification board. Pay close attention to local labor requirements as well, such as those from unions. Contact each and/or use their online resources to determine which are relevant.

Multiple jurisdictions

When operating a business across multiple jurisdictions, you must check what's needed in each individual jurisdiction. The commerce clause of the U.S. Constitution encourages the regulatory systems not to inhibit interstate commerce through unnecessary regulatory requirements, but it can still be very complex. For example, I represented a trucking company that had business operations in 36 states. After it was all said and done, we had to deal with four business organizations, nine insurance policies and almost sixty different licenses, just for the business and corporate officers.

Regulations

Regulations are rules that trigger punishments if you break them. Punishments are civil, meaning they might be monetary fines or prohibition from taking specific actions, but violations are not criminal offenses.

Regulations are closely tied to the licensing we just discussed. Your business's regulations will come from your industry, probably including multiple jurisdictions and multiple levels.

Your business will have regulations or rules in all its aspects: environmental, financial, tax, advertising, Internet, public policy, etc. Ignorance is never an excuse; it is not a valid defense to a violation. If you are unsure or do not know, then ask or research. Yes, there are quite a few regulations out there, but they are not hiding. The system is designed to be known about and complied with.

Why the licenses and regulations?

The two primary purposes behind licensing and regulation are public policy and economic benefits. The public policy purpose states that if your business's goal is to make a profit, it may choose that profit over the greater good of the community. For example, consider the harmful chemicals and emissions which many manufacturing industries continue to produce and improperly dispose of. Until the government enacts regulatory standards for allowable chemical emissions and proper disposal, the manufacturers may choose practices based on savings rather than the public good.

But not all policies go against the potential profits of companies. The economic benefit purpose states that for the benefit of consumers and the overall market, the government should regulate as necessary to encourage fair marketplace competition. This policy has led to the break-up of monopolies in specific industries, creating separate competing entities, like the historic breakup of AT&T in the U.S.

Taxes

No doubt, taxes are one of the most critical aspects of business planning and operations. It's sad but true: improper bookkeeping, record maintenance and tax planning will break many new businesses.

The process starts with implementing and reinforcing the procedures for proper and accurate bookkeeping. Money is one big reason you are in business, and it is what keeps you there. Bookkeeping is not about efficiency, it is about accuracy and forming a clear picture for future action.

All this rests on professional records maintenance: This includes the checks and balances of having information recorded in multiple locations by multiple people. Have a backup for everything offsite, scan paper copies, etc.

Most small business owners do not actually understand or utilize their financial information. When I ask, "What are your monthly fixed costs? What is your monthly breakeven point?" I usually get a dazed look. Or responses like, "Last month was a good month" or "I have no idea." Answers like these mean that the owner is basically flying blind financially, and not just about taxes. The amount of debt, the business's liquidity, its 90-day forecasted budget and other key measures of business health are all unknowns.

You can avoid nasty surprises if you regularly spend quality time with your accountant or bookkeeper. Get into the numbers until you understand them, until they speak to you. The time you spend will be worth its weight in gold in the end.

So as we leave the topic of licenses, regulation and taxes, we come back to the initial point. Get your ducks in a row on these matters, ensure that records and compliance are completely reliable, and then, plow back into the business you dreamed of, knowing you have not neglected these technical requirements that can sabotage your success.

M.R.M.

Insurance—A Risk-Management Tool

If you think of insurance this way,
its cost may seem less onerous.

IN THE LAST SECTION, we looked at obligations you and your business have toward governing entities. Now let's look at an obligation that you, as an entrepreneur and business owner, have to your own business. You need to protect it against events that could harm or even destroy it. In effect, that's what insurance is all about.

Insurance allows you to transfer risk to your insurer, in exchange for the compensation you pay to him (your insurance premium). You buy insurance, in the form of policies, from licensed insurance companies. The insurance policy may be general or specific. There are often options, modifications and riders (amendments available for extra cost) available for policies that allow you to customize the policy for your specific business needs. The most common of these are deductible amounts and total policy amounts.

Business insurance comes in several varieties:

- General Liability—very broad coverage, a necessity for every business. It covers the costs of legal defense or repairing damages related to harmful events or claims against you, your employees and your products. Such insurance only covers accidents and negligence. It does not cover willful actions or gross negligence.

- Property—covers real and personal property owned by the business. This is specific insurance and is limited to the replacement of the property only, in the event of the destruction or loss related to a specifically covered occurrence. You must verify what types of risks are covered. For example, some policies put all damage to property on one policy, in contrast with coastal areas, where flood and/or windstorm insurance is often only covered if an additional policy is purchased. Note that property insurance does not protect from loss of income or operations related to the destruction of property.

- Casualty—general coverage related to specific occurrences. It is very similar to general liability insurance. In addition to covering for negligence, it could be used to cover events like theft, political risk, earthquakes or shipwrecks.

- Flood—a specific type of property insurance related to flood damage. Note that this coverage may not be available in all areas, and will only cover property actually damaged by floodwaters.

- Terrorism/Acts of War—covers losses related to terrorism or war risk. This type may not be necessary for the average business. Government contractors and other businesses conducting business operations in high-risk environments use it.

- Business Owners'/Income/Business Interruption—coverage related to replacing the revenues and income of a business in the event of a loss. It may be bundled with other specific coverages and customized to the business.

- Vehicle—covers events related the operation of motor vehicles. This may include company vehicles operated for business purposes and also employees' personal vehicles operated for work purposes. This is high risk insurance, with significant variability among insurance policy options.

- Workers' Compensation—coverage related to employee injuries on the job. The insurance will provide income replacement and medical coverage to the employee. Workers' Compensation insurance is mandatory in most jurisdictions in the U.S. Note that this does not cover any effects on the business for decreased revenues due to the limitations of the employee.

- Professional Liability/Errors and Omissions—coverage related to the defense and damages of claims for improper professional service by a licensed professional or business. Note that this type of risk is usually excluded from all general insurance policies, so to get this protection you must purchase a separate policy.

- Product Liability—coverage related to claims for damages related to your product. Certain customers (e.g., a nation-wide chain store that buys your baby toys) sometimes will require you, their supplier, to purchase this coverage for stated minimum amounts, and even to name them as beneficiaries.

- Directors' and Officers' Insurance—coverage to protect the directors and officers of a business, should they suffer any loss or expenses for legal defense based on their actions within the business.

- Data Breach—coverage that protects the business in case a breach of confidential data occurs.

- Transactional—coverage related to risk on a specific transaction. Examples include insuring a shipment or title insurance on a property transfer.

- Homeowners'—general liability insurance for the business owner's personal home. If you are a home-based business owner, you need to verify whether your business can be covered on your existing homeowners' policy. Also ensure that the operation of your home-based business does not void your homeowners' policy.

- Renters/Contents—coverage related to only the contents or equipment within leased or rented premises. If you store your products in a third party's warehouse, you may be required to insure your stock against damage from fire, water, etc. while it's there. You may want to insure it even if it's not required; do the math to see what's reasonable.

- Disability/Life/Key Person (or Keyman)—specific coverage related to the business's loss of income in the event of the death or disability of a key person within the organization. This type of insurance is often integrated into a business's buy/sell agreement or in succession planning. Note that this coverage may require key people not to travel together, to minimize risks.

- Umbrella—general coverage that supplements all other existing policies. Think of it like your safety net in case any of the other insurance policies are insufficient.

As a business owner you must effectively cover both the business and yourself to insure that claims agains one cannot impact the other. Business owners are very often the preferred targets for conmen and fraudulent claims. Also, please remember that the insurance agent and company are for-profit businesses. You need to understand what your risks are and then verify that those are insured against.

M.R.M.

"The Name's Bond—Surety Bond"

You might be licensed and insured,
but are you bonded?

OCCASIONALLY, a small business, especially one performing contracting services, is asked to bond its work in advance. In some places, certain types of contractors are required to be bonded.*

Simply put, a bond is a financial guarantee that you will honor a business contract. Sometimes referred to as a *surety bond*, a bond is a promise by a third party to pay if a vendor does not fulfill its valid obligations under a contract. There are various types of bonds, such as license bonds, performance bonds, bid bonds, indemnity bonds, and payment bonds.

- A *license* bond is required by some localities for certain businesses. In some cases, you pay the locality directly rather than obtaining a bond.

- A *performance* bond is a guarantee that you will perform work in accordance with the terms of a contract.

- A *bid* bond is a guarantee you will perform work if you win a bidding contest.

- An *indemnity* bond promises to reimburse losses incurred if you fail to perform or if you fail to pay other vendors in the fulfillment of a contact.

- A *payment* bond promises that you will pay all subcontractors and material providers utilized in the performance of a contract.

*This section first appeared in our book, *Starting a Business* (Nova Vista Publishing, ISBN 978-90-77256-36-7).

It is important to remember that a bond is *not* an insurance policy. A bond only provides assurance that the contracted work will be satisfactorily completed. For example, your bond will not pay for property damage or personal injury resulting from your work. For this, you need conventional insurance coverage.

A simple Google search will list companies that provide bonding services under *surety bonds* in your area. In general, bonding companies will only provide bond coverage up to an amount that you can cover with existing liquid assets.

Before you purchase a bond from any bonding company, have the bond documentation reviewed by your attorney and ensure that you understand exactly what the bond can and cannot protect against. This will benefit both you and your customer.

S.G.

How to Reorganize or Restructure Your Business

They say change is one constant in business...

WHY WOULD YOU reorganize or restructure your business? There are many reasons. They all share the goal of making your business more profitable and better positioned for success in the future.

When you start a business, the last thing you might picture is turning it upside down and inside out. Yet a smart entrepreneur doesn't take much for granted. You start detecting things that aren't working well, or opportunities you're not set up to seize... that's when it's time to think about change.

You are right to think that restructuring and reorganizing are management tools, not legal issues per se. But imbedded in many actions you might take here are vital legal implications. Don't neglect to bring your attorney into your planning sessions if you are undertaking significant change. She may recognize things you need to consider or do that will save you many future headaches.

Reasons to restructure a business

- **Strategic Repositioning** New strategies may require changes to the core business, moving into new or developing markets and out of saturated ones, developing new product lines, etc. This reshaping reflects and supports a fundamental change in the business's long-term goals, which renders the current business structure obsolete. Note that this may require new business leadership, so don't put blinders on.

- **Crisis Management** Often this is a swift, urgent reaction. It could be as extreme as a business liquidation bankruptcy, the relocation of manufacturing related to growing instability in the area, or downsizing by laying off 50 percent of the workforce to get back to profitability.

- **Negotiation with Stakeholders** Topics could include buyouts, shuffling of positions or recapitalization in preparation for the future.

- **New Operational Methods** Changing to a new and better way to get the same work done more efficiently (running the business in three shifts instead of one); adopting a new management style or culture (implementing Six Sigma); or embracing new technology (since every sales rep now carries a tablet and can prepare estimates on site, we no longer require dedicated estimators).

- **Litigation and Compliance** Suppose that in relation to a lawsuit, audit or other inspection, deficiencies were discovered within the business organization that must be corrected. Compliance can be forward looking as well. There may be significant new regulatory or legislative requirements on the horizon, and you want your business to be the leader in implementing changes to comply.

- **Mergers, Acquisitions and Sales of Businesses** In the eat-or-be-eaten business world these things happen all the time. Merger is joining with another company, and then merging your organizations together to from a stronger business. Acquisition is the assimilation of one business into another. Sales could include all or part of a business, or just specific aspects of the business, like a data base, intellectual property, or only one division.

- **Insolvency** In this situation, change could include debt settlement or negotiation before a bankruptcy is filed. Public policy encourages businesses to be profitable, and therefore the insolvency process is designed to reorganize unprofitable or unstable businesses for greater long-term economic benefits.

If you have determined that you have a reason and need to restructure or reorganize, then you must determine whether the changes will be primarily internal or external. Be aware that with any reorganization, the changes will always affect the business internally and externally. Each situation will be unique, and you will need to analyze the situation and consider many factors beyond the items listed here. These are meant as simple guiding principle to get you moving in the right direction.

Internal reorganizations

These reshape the inner workings of your business: its leadership, management, operations, profit and regulation. There's a natural process you can follow:

- Identify the purpose for the reorganization

- Develop various options to achieve that purpose and evaluate each one's costs and benefits

- Select the best reorganization model available

- Prepare a detailed plan for the reorganization (see more on this below)

- Clearly communicate it to all members of the organization or team affected and others indirectly affected

- Assign actions, giving specific reasons for the change required and detailed descriptions of to-do's and deadlines

- Stay on top of the change process until it's complete, as it's your job to maintain organizational cohesion and confidence in the business while changes are implemented

As you move through the process, remember that all members of the team have a stake in the success of the business, and put yourself in their shoes. What would motivate them? Freedom from frustration and inefficiency? Dividends? Continued work and a paycheck?

The importance of planning and tracking changes

A business reorganization is an extremely resource-intensive process, consuming time, money and labor. It is critical that you take your time and move through the process in a deliberate manner. Unless there is an impending crisis, the planning phase can seem extremely slow and detail oriented. Use any and all available outside resources to assist in the process, whether that is a professional consultant or hiring temporary labor for moving items physically. That will allow you to focus your energies on the business, where it needs to be.

The two most common mistakes I see in the planning phase sound like this:

- "That's not what I told them to do." Put your plans in writing and be prepared to say things many times. Your documentation does not need to be fancy, but it must be crystal clear. Place it in a centralized, accessible source for all reorganization information. That could be on your company's server, or in the lunch room—make sure it's kept up to date and encourage everyone to check on progress frequently. Use graphics, pictures, flow charts, maps, slides—whatever it takes. The goal is just to get the same message and a track on progress out to all organization members.

- "Well, I started it, but we never quite finished." Most people work better with deadlines. As part of your plan, include a timeline that states when certain milestones and tasks need to be done. You owe it to the business to fully complete the plan, since the reorganization might not work as expected unless it's finished. I've had clients blush and confess, "I went through all the trouble to amend my corporate structure, but never filed the documents."

Implementation

Once the plan is complete and everyone knows what to do, go ahead and get it done. Watch out for unintended effects. Assist as necessary to ensure all deadlines are met and make changes as necessary. Ensure you are complying with all local rules or professional guidelines. For example, some unions have requirements that employees are told who their supervisor is within a certain period after hiring or after there's a change in supervision. If layoffs are involved, emphasize that the business and remaining employees' jobs are now more financially secure. Pay particular attention to employee interactions with clients to ensure they convey confidence in the business.

Just about every business goes through internal reorganizations. The process need only be as formal as you think necessary. But it must be thorough. The more thorough you are, the more your business will gain from the changes. Suppose you need to reassign job duties in an office. You could do that by simply saying, "Allen, you're going to answer the phone." Or you could explain why this change is needed and what you hope it will accomplish, then provide Allen with a job duties description, a copy of the phone greeting he should use, a summary of likely questions and responses, and a printed form to use for messages taken. Which scenario will produce the best performance from Allen?

External reorganizations

External reorganizations focus on how your business works facing the outside world: its business structure (sole proprietor? partnership?), customer and vendor relations, market interactions, sales and marketing activity, growth model, billing, accounts receivable, accounts payable, brand value, etc.

Once the business has identified the need for reorganization, the same planning process as for an internal reorganization can begin. But because external reorganization may impact many participants beyond your control, it will be more complex, and some of the players may not be influenced as easily as your employees. Planning considerations include legal and other regulations, taxes, liabilities, and a wealth of other aspects of your business. Further, you must consider the impact of changes on external relationships and responsibilities, including market and contractual relationships with clients, suppliers, debtors, creditors, etc., before selecting the appropriate process.

Debt-driven external reorganizations focus on debt, collections, liquidity and insolvency. Planning considerations are driven by the willingness of creditors to settle, restructure or reduce debts owed; the desire of the business to continue operations; and the individual liability of stakeholders for business debts. In the U.S., a Chapter 11 business reorganizational bankruptcy, or the threat of it, is an immensely powerful tool available to businesses in continuing operations. The alternative is a Chapter 7 liquidation bankruptcy, or the local jurisdiction's statutes on cessation of business operations. These aim at a termination of the business entity.

Appropriate planning and assistance are critical for success. Your attorney very likely can help with her broader base of experience with clients who have come through similar situations, as well as representing your business's interest if you need to renegotiate terms, develop new agreements, or wind down the business.

Pitfalls to avoid

There are some common issues that cause the most trouble in completing a business reorganization.

- First, objections by stakeholders (anybody with an interest in the change), whether a majority or minority, which can affect the process.

- Resistance by management or employees, which can be a respectful difference of opinion, general resistance to change, or malicious actions with ulterior motives. They can derail a perfectly reasonable plan.

- Financial or tax consequences to particular individuals. These can make reorganization difficult or impossible.

- Corporate documents or regulations that prevent or forbid the reorganization desired.

- Current operations or contracts that can also block reorganization.

I mention these things not to deter you from launching a well-planned reorganization, but to ensure you are aware of the magnitude of responsibilities that face you as you progress through the process. Being aware of them and handling each challenge effectively is the mark of an excellent leader.

Documentation

As with any discussion involving an attorney, I must remind you about documenting everything. Depending on how your business is set up, you will have some level of requirement to record (keep a written record of) major decisions made, who made the decision, if or why they had the power to do so and details on notifications of all necessary parties about this change. Have you updated all regulatory agencies? Have you updated all license registrations? Are there any follow-on changes required, such as amendments to previously filed documents?

In short, your business, like your baby, is going to grow and change over time. You cannot ignore this. You must plan for change, including your attorney in the change team as needed. In the long run, the more effort you put into keeping your business properly organized in support of your goals, the more rewards and profit you will see in the end.

M.R.M.

Starting at Step... Two?

*Think about your customer's experience from
a legal point of view and profit from it.*

FOR THOSE OF YOU who read our first book, *Starting a Business*, you'll recall that we explained that fledgling entrepreneurs all pass through a basic two-part progression. Step One is creating your exciting new venture and actually getting it off the ground. Step Two, how you actually run it, will determine your success or failure. That's particularly true when you consider your customers' experiences in dealing with your company.

Know what you don't know

Faced with high failure rates, a new business needs all the help it can get. Two areas, accounting and law, are typically black boxes for entrepreneurs. There's a reason why financial and legal professionals are required to have so much education, knowledge and training. Knowing what you don't know is the first step to succeeding, especially long-term.

Think like a customer—that tells you what to do

No matter what type of business you have (or are planning to launch), one of your first research projects will be to learn everything you can about your potential customers. What are their needs? What are their buying habits? What do they expect when problems arise? What does the competition do? How can you maintain your customer base over time? What promises and guarantees will earn customers' trust and confidence?

With your results in hand, you need to set up policies that address your customers' needs but that are also legal. A lawyer can support these efforts in many ways. Here are just a few examples of legal matters she can advise you about:

- Warranties, written guarantees, renewals and updates

- Refund and return policies

- Help desk, post-sale service and user-support websites

- Contracts, agreements, invoices, work and purchase orders

- Packaging, product disclaimers, information and warnings

- Contests, drawings, customer loyalty programs

The last thing you want is disputes with your customers. If you've established correct, customer-friendly ways of doing basic business, your customers will come to trust your company and feel loyal to your brand. An up-front approach provides an "open book" feeling for both parties.

Taking the time to properly establish these legal baselines can have a positive effect on sales, marketing, and advertising initiatives too. It will even boost word-of-mouth referrals. Entrepreneurs who understand the importance of delivering on every element of a customer experience through a well-defined legal approach are usually the ones who defy most odds and beat the competition. And don't forget that every day, your lawyer sees things that work and don't work in other clients' businesses. She can become your ad-hoc business advisor with insights that go beyond just legal matters.

Now, go run your biz like a pro

Empowering your employees to interact with customers in all phases of your sales process, from initial contact through negotiations to the final sale, becomes much easier with legal documentation in place for all to access. It protects both parties during each stage of the process and leaves little to the imagination on both sides. It's also easier to train new hires, as the written policies and terms are established and in place.

Additionally, elements such as warranties and return policies, if drawn up properly, will allow you to compare yours with competitors'. Use these points in marketing and advertising campaigns to differentiate your offering as well. Showcasing your "money back guarantees" and other equivalent components can lead to more sales.

These principles have been a way of life in everything I've ever done as an entrepreneur. I'm convinced that attorneys can contribute at every step of your business's existence.

M.P.

CHAPTER III

Operating Activities

Running the Show: An Overview

*Your attorney can support your success in many
ways. Some of them may surprise you.*

YOU PLAY MANY ROLES AS AN ENTREPRENEUR. You may be a founder, a funder, a leader, a major contributor to your business's output of goods or services, a face your company shows the world, a boss… the list goes on and on.

One role you may not recognize as clearly as those is that of custodian. You are responsible for the protection of the business entity itself, its owners or operators, investors, employees, outsourced organizations, as well as the consumers it serves. It's a heavy load. But your attorney can help you carry it.

Laying the foundation

A good attorney can guide you through the important steps of laying a rock-solid foundation, beginning with input on your initial business plan and advising on the structure of your business (or its expansion). And once you're off and running, she can help you make strategic moves essential for growth and profit. Helping you to also thwart potential legal setbacks, a top-notch legal pro can be essential in keeping the biz on the upswing.

An attorney is a vital piece of the small business puzzle. Whether it's sketching out a company on a piece of paper or buying an existing one from someone else, your attorney should be a key player, ensuring that the business is in proper legal working order from the onset.

The attorneys I have worked with as an entrepreneur have always operated like a complete support system to me. Most of my businesses have been (and are all currently) small, so I've never needed an in-house attorney. Instead, I commission various lawyers or firms to work on specific projects. It works great for me, and I count it as one reason I've enjoyed a satisfying success record.

Day-to-day aspects

I took a look through my legal files before starting to write this section. The variety and extent of projects surprised even me. Here is a partial list.

- Business plan reviews
- Strategic planning
- Forming a corporation
- Lawsuits and litigation
- Legal correspondence
- Selling a business
- Buying a business
- Liability risks
- Asset protection
- Investor documents and packets
- Partnership and operating agreements
- Warranties, written guarantees, and related policies
- Refunds and return policies
- Contracts and agreements (a huge array)
- Invoices and work or purchase orders
- Packaging and product disclaimers
- Hiring, compensation, and termination matters
- Employee manuals and training guides
- Real estate, including rental, lease, purchase and sales agreements
- International business advice and referrals

And that list is just my personal one. As you can see, very few resemble the classic picture of an attorney addressing a courtroom on your behalf (though that could happen one day). The fact is that as an entrepreneur, you constantly face decisions and the need to act to ensure your own, the company's and your customers' best interests. You need that legal support system I mentioned earlier.

Signatures are signals

How do I decide when I need that support? I've got a simple rule: If I need to sign something, I ask myself if this is something I need advice on. Of course, there are things like credit card purchases and routine tasks like signing checks or purchase orders that don't count, but if any other type of transaction or document of any kind requires a signature from me, and of course if there will be any type of liability involved, I ask my attorney to review it.

One benefit of this approach is that over time, I've gotten a good informal legal education. I prefer to work with attorneys who teach me how to think, explaining what the law means, how a process works, or why they favor a certain strategy. Gradually I've gotten to be a much better legal consumer, asking better questions and spotting opportunities or pitfalls with a much better sense of the business and legal implications.

This education even translates into how I act in doing my business, particularly regarding what I say and don't say. Promising a customer or employee something you are not later capable of or willing to uphold could also put you into that courtroom we pictured before. It's for these reasons an attorney should be involved when you're operating outside your routine comfort zone.

The future is actually here today—pay attention!

Other legal issues with huge implications can pop up with little or no advance warning. What if you your top-selling product is about to be outlawed due to new environmental laws? What if your city wants to put a prison next to the day care center you are about to buy? What if new hiring or pay practices are about to become law, and your growth plan is based on the current ones? There are countless threats your business could be susceptible to every single day. Your attorney can serve as an extra pair of eyes and ears working on your behalf to spot upcoming issues. Here are just a few that could be looming:

- New national, international or professional regulations on products or services

- Local municipality decisions

- New environmental laws or restrictions

- Local zoning, building, or operational changes

- National product recalls

- Wage regulations

- Insurance requirements

- Hiring and firing law changes

- Product or intellectual property infringements

I have faced a number of these issues in my career, and fully expect to experience other challenges in the future. This is where a seasoned attorney can step in and save the day. So the moral of this story is simple: Expert legal advice and guidance is vital for long-term success. From the day-to-day operational questions, to the quick review of a single document, to full representation in a courtroom on your behalf, an attorney is your legal lifeline. Together you can keep your business and yourself humming along on all fronts.

M.P.

Internal Documents You Really Need

*Build your company's document
archive to prevent headaches.*

PAPERWORK, PAPERWORK, PAPERWORK. Few entrepreneurs love it—I mean, the paperwork *behind* your business, even if your business's core service is to handle others' paperwork! Certainly, unless you are one of those gifted organizers driven by the need for order, you didn't start your business with paperwork as your driving force.

Still, you do have a business to run. Often when I review required and recommended documents with startup clients, their eyes glaze over and they look away. Yet you know what? Even in the most creative, crazy businesses, the ones that maintain control over documents seem to survive better than their disorganized counterparts.

I realize each business, small or large, each management team and each operational process is unique. And often in the very early days, creativity and free-wheeling invention is the prevailing style. But here's the thing: There are countless businesses ready to sell you a T-shirt, design advanced electronic widgets or provide elder care, but there are only a few startups that have been extremely successful at it. A certain degree of their success can be tied back to their documentation. Tough as it may be for you to hear, the real businesspeople among all the starry-eyed starters just know and accept that the devil can be in the details. Do you want to sink your ship because you didn't attend to paperwork?

This section and the next are designed to provide a general overview of some of the most common documents that businesses need to keep under control. Every jurisdiction, industry and business has individual requirements about what you must collect, analyze, review and maintain, some of which may not be included on this list. As a business owner, decide if you should consult appropriate professionals or resources to set up and maintain processes to manage them.

Also, note that these lists are created from an attorney's perspective. My primary role is to protect your business from liability and ensure continued operations, so my focus here is not efficiency in particular—there are experts in our Resource section who deal with that. So let's take a look at your paperwork needs. In this section we'll deal with internal documents; in the next, external documents.

Internal documentation

Internal business documents are those used primarily within your business to start and run it. Generally, they are not disclosed to outsiders. These internal documents may include your secret formula, employee contracts, internal process maps, decision-making process documents, etc. It will help you to think of them as divided into four areas: formation and structure, planning, operations, and transition.

Business Formation and Structure Documents

Articles of Formation Depending on the type of business entity you selected when you founded the business, these could be articles of incorporation, partnership or organization documents, to name a few. They are almost always required in order to set up a business. Typically they set the business structure, name key personnel and duty positions, identify the nature of the business and more. The required content can vary greatly between jurisdictions.

Bylaws or Operating Agreement These are the specific procedures, rules and regulations, as set by the business, to guide the business's ongoing operations and management. They can include provisions on funding, ownership, distributions, tax liability, decision-making, liquidation, voting rights and much more. These documents are extremely important in businesses with multiple individuals involved in the startup or management, since items like profit distributions and decision-making are a major source of internal disputes. You may make terms as specific as necessary. If you don't have such a document, your jurisdiction will most likely have default rules that will be applied if necessary. It's far better to call the shots pro-actively by drawing up your bylaws when you found your business.

Corporate Minutes The written record or documentation of meetings. It will most likely be required by your individual jurisdiction and also by your bylaws that certain meetings, debates and decisions be documented and maintained as an ongoing record. They generally do not have to be verbatim transcripts, but just summary notes. I recommend you select a format that fits your business, keep it simple, record all key company activities and include details for each recording.

Ownership Certificates These could include stock certificates for corporations, membership certificates for limited liability companies (LLCs) or partnership certificates for limited partnerships. The certificates serve as an important record for business ledgers and registers. They also increase the business's reputability by providing the holders with tangible documentation representing their ownership and stake in the business.

Tax Identification Number and Other Initial Tax Declarations Your tax ID number is the initial separation between you, the private individual who is the business founder, and the non-human entity which is the business. It ensures distinct treatment of the business revenues from those of the owner. Along with this unique number comes the requirement to file and maintain business specific accounting and books. These requirements can be made by multiple jurisdictions, such as local, state and federal. You will also need to make and document a number of elections (choices) right away, such as your business tax year and specific tax elections (like S-Corporation tax status, non-profit, etc.) These may vary by jurisdiction.

Business Planning Documents

Business Plan The written plan to make your business successful. The detail, length and areas included in your business plan should reflect your business's needs and complexity. If you are seeking financing or some type of regulatory approval, the plan will need to be more specific in certain areas. Generally, these documents will include the business goals, product description, product distinction, market analysis, leadership team, marketing plan, opportunities, challenges, initial budget, revenue forecasts and break-even point. A business plan is a living document that should be updated at specific periods or when major changes occur.

Mission and Strategic Vision Statement This declares the goals for your business, outlining your business's purpose, philosophies and objectives. It should be short and to the point. The mission statement should include your primary market, contribution to that market and your distinction. The mission statement and vision for the company should guide the company in decision-making and strategic planning. As with your business plan, it's important to review this document periodically and to adjust it if significant shifts cause you to redirect your business.

Forecasts of Sales, Cash Flow, Revenues, etc. Forecasting is the formal process of anticipating future business. Many consider this more of an art than a science. The two primary methods used are *qualitative* (subjective and based on opinions of professionals) or *quantitative* (based on past data). While the process to make forecasts varies greatly from business to business, each one must do it at some level. The more you document these forecasts and are thus able to improve your future forecasting, the more efficient your business will be. In addition, these documents may be required for loan or regulatory purposes. In that case, the appropriate documents can usually be prepared with the aid of a financial professional or financial software.

Insurance Policies As discussed in the section on insurance, there are a number of risks that you want to insure against. Your policies are the contracts that actually transfer the risk. The policy only covers what is specifically described, so make sure that these documents cover the risks you want to address. Here's a good tip: play the "what if" game with your insurance agent. Run through a number of scenarios and ask her to show you exactly where in the contract you are covered for that risk and explain how the process would work if that event were to occur. Ask for adjustments if you are not satisfied. (Later, if unfortunately the event does happen, you'll be better prepared to respond and not have false expectations.)

Buy/Sell Agreements These agreements are also known as business wills or buyout agreements. I strongly recommend them for multi-owner businesses in which the owners actively participate in business operations. They specify the terms and conditions related to an ownership change, such as the death of an owner, buyout, retirement, divorce, sale, etc. These agreements are often funded through insurance products to ensure minimal impact on the business operations and to the other owners.

Incapacity, Death and Trust Documents These relate to the personal documents of the primary owners and operators of a business. They should be reviewed and updated, to ensure minimal disruption to the business or appropriate planning. Incapacity is a disability or injury that renders the individual unable to work or make decisions. The planning considerations and documents used here could include powers of attorney, disability insurance and succession planning in the operating agreement. Planning considerations for the death of an owner include buy-sell agreements, wills, probate, trusts and other estate-planning considerations. While these documents are not directly part of the business, they must be reviewed and properly documented to ensure the long-term success of the business.

Business Operations Documents

Human resources documents

Employment Agreements This is a contract between the business, as the employer, and the employee, for the purpose of defining the terms of the relationship, such as pay, performance measures and duration. Depending on the employee's position and your jurisdiction, this may or may not be necessary. When in doubt, write it out.

Non-Disclosure/Confidentiality Agreements These common agreements may be addenda to an employment contract or done as a stand-alone agreement. They are used whenever a person related to the business (an employee, contractor, consultant, potential partner, etc.) will have access to sensitive information. They put the other party on notice that there will be a significant penalty if this information is disclosed outside the business. Often the other party is contracting for and consenting to additional punishments if they violate the confidentiality. At some levels, these agreements can be mutually binding (as when your chemical lab wants an equipment designer to create a new gadget, and you must disclose some proprietary information in order for the designer to see what you need).

Non-Compete Agreements These also may be addenda to an employment contract or a stand-alone agreement. They relate to future competition in certain professions, geographic areas, markets or industries. These are very specific and can vary by jurisdiction and industry as to what is allowed.

Employee Manual and Policies The basic human resources manual that your business should have. It spells out all of your business's basic policies on subjects such as paid time off, vacations, personal phone use at work, email and internet use, drug testing, smoking areas, harassment reporting, etc. The policies should be accurately described and evenly enforced. Regard this as a living document that should be updated periodically, particularly if employment laws change.

Your employee manual is very important in protecting your business from employment-related lawsuits. Even if you only employ one person, you need to have one. Outsource human resource companies can provide a customized manual on a project-fee basis.

Pay, Commissions, Bonuses, Incentives, Raises You are in business to make a profit and your employees are there for compensation. The compensation plan needs to be simple, clear and evenly applied to all employees. You may include this information in the employee manual or as part of the individual employment agreements. Compensation is considered to be the top motivator of employees, and conversely the top demotivator if it is unclear or unfairly applied.

Management Documents

Business Hierarchy, Operational Structure This document (sometimes including a graphic called an organizational chart, or org chart) describes exactly who works for whom and how units or departments are structured and relate to each other. Even in a small company, it is very important to have a clear chain of command, with reporting and accountability structures in place. It is also very important to maintain this hierarchy to some extent throughout the business. In employment-related litigation, cases about hierarchy and structure are common: "Did you know who to report that to?" Protect your business and document its structure and hierarchy, and make sure your employees know how it works.

Employee Performance Evaluations These should be standardized forms, used throughout the business. They may contain both objective and subjective criteria, so long as the criteria are fairly applied. These forms are very relevant in the context of termination, discrimination claims and pay disputes. Performance evaluations and forms should be completed regularly, on a schedule outlined in the employee manual. It's a best practice to have both the employee and supervisor initial and date the form used for each discussion.

Job Descriptions and Performance Standards These very important documents are individually designed or may be part of the employee manual. The documents clearly lay out exactly what is expected of each employee and the requirements of each job. They set the standard operating procedures for which your business could be held liable and become very relevant in any negligence or general liability suits.

Procedures, Flow Charts Operations procedures or flow charts are just a more detailed extension of the performance standards described above. They define what standard procedures are for a task in your company. The procedures can be as simple as the telephone greeting to a complete manufacturing process. Flow charts are graphical representations of the procedures. In the event of a problem, having this documentation could protect your business from liability, if you need to prove that an employee deviated from standard procedure.

Quantitative Measurements and Tools These are the ongoing internal measurements you use to analyze your business. They need to be tied directly and accurately to many of the other documents discussed in this section. For example, your business may run weekly or monthly sales reports. Is there a procedure on exactly how to run these reports? Are these reports broken down by individual salespeople? Are the results of these reports tied to their employee evaluations or pay?

Accounting Documents

Standard Books These are your internal bookkeeping and accounting documents. There are many software programs to help you create and complete them, or you can delegate the work to an accountant. From the liability perspective, you must follow generally accepted accounting principles. Always consider the following questions: Who is ultimately responsible for these records? Is there a checks and balances system in place to ensure that no single person has complete control of the accounting? Otherwise, there may be no one to catch mistakes or spot potential theft.

Invoices, Ordering, Inter-Business Communications These are the internal documents that help your business track and manage its business processes. The items tracked may not have any tax or cash effect on the accounting, but could be just as relevant to the success of the overall business. For example, think about the internal delivery schedule for various components to be assembled prior to shipment or sale. Documenting and managing this process is key. From the liability perspective, if you have this clearly documented, then you should be covered in case of a breakdown in the system.

Marketing Documents

Clients and Potential Client Tracking These are the internal documents, notes and information that you may collect and store on clients, potential clients and previous clients. This information should be handled securely. Thoroughly documented client lists are business assets and can carry significant value.

Reports and Measurements of ROI These internal reports relate to revenues, sales, profits, etc. They may all be the same as the taxable events documents discussed in the accounting section, or they could serve a different purpose. Often, business contracts have payment escalators based on the results of these reports. Therefore, it is critical that the reports are accurate. For example, many commercial leases have a portion of the rent that is variable and based on gross revenues. It is imperative to ensure all parties affected understand how these numbers will be calculated and reported.

If you are feeling a little swamped by all this talk of documentation, bear in mind that if you have not started up yet, you can build your document archive step by step as your business takes shape and grows. If you are up and running now, and lack certain documents, it may be best to identify what is missing and make up a schedule for completing the needed documentation over a reasonable period of time. Like any sizeable piece of work, it will seem less daunting if it's cut down to smaller steps.

M.R.M.

External Documents You Really Need

More docs for the archive, this time looking outward.

UNLIKE THE DOCUMENTS WE'VE JUST CONSIDERED, external business documents are used outside of your business, when it interacts with other entities, individuals or regulatory agencies. These documents could include contracts, letters, tax filings, collection matters, and transitional business documents.

External documentation

Some of the major external business documents include these:

Outside Contracts As we've noted repeatedly, contracts will cover just about everything you do as a business. These contracts will need to meet the specific requirements of your jurisdiction related to that issue. Be wary of "standard contracts" that people have always used and always read the fine print.

Order Forms and Confirmations These can become critical in your business at any given moment. The key issues are: When is the contract formed? And when does the risk of loss shift?

The nature of your business helps shape the interpretation. Imagine that a customer places an order and then cancels it. There is a difference when you compare the impact at Sea Breeze Yachts, a company that builds high-end custom yachts for a very small market, as opposed to Super Scoop, an ice cream shop. At what point in the process is the business able to make a claim against the client who cancels? Who is at risk if the product is damaged during production? How does this change if you are a supplier that provides ongoing building materials to only a select few customers? At what point does an order become a contract? How are the orders for one job related to orders for another job, both for the same customer? The answers should be spelled out in the master contract and your order and confirmation documents.

Invoices These are the ongoing billings. You must consider your business's liquidity, cash flow model and the industry in determining your company's invoicing policy, as there are different standards in each case. Another major consideration is ensuring the accuracy of the invoices you create, as you could be found to have waived part of the amount due if you invoice incorrectly. The invoice and payment periods should be dictated in your initial business contract.

Receipts These document both funds paid out and received. Although you would think a business would automatically capture them, receipt problems are very common, either because they were not provided, got lost, or the receipt was not documented properly. Stay on top of them, down to the last scrap on your petty cash expenses, to be prepared for audits or to identify costs later.

Credit Agreements Most business owners automatically say they do not offer credit. But how many of your clients pay you up front, in full, every time? A majority of industries do not operate this way. If you are in one of them, then you are indirectly extending credit. Both indirect and direct credit agreements should be documented, either in the original business contract or as a separate agreement. If your business is functioning as a creditor, see that it is fairly compensated for this risk.

Collections Going right along with those credit agreements are collections. How do you get money that customers owe you but have not paid? This process may include letters, late fees, liens, demands, penalties and even lawsuits. The remedies available will be based on your business contract and then on the laws of your jurisdiction. You must also be aware of consumer protection laws that limit and regulate the collection of debts, so as not to violate the law or impact the collectability of your debt.

Mortgages/Deeds/Leases These are documents related to land and commercial space as well as equipment for your business. They can be very complex and long-term documents, so it is best to seek professional assistance when you need to execute one. They are also one of the most common areas of dispute in business litigation. You must know what your business is getting into and how that could affect your long-term plans. (See pages 50-54 for more on real estate deals.)

Letterhead and disclosures These vary from industry to industry. You'll see them at the end of emails, where the sender has a statement that says, "This is confidential information, and if you receive it in error, please destroy," etc. If they are necessary for your business, you may need to include them in all your communications. There may also be disclosures that you must include on every communication of a certain type. For example, "This is an attempt to collect a debt." These disclosures should be reviewed with your attorney and maintained as part of your ongoing business compliance.

Tax I know, I have already harped enough on proper bookkeeping and accounting. The next step in the process is filing all the appropriate tax forms at the correct intervals. These could be on your sales, salaries or other periodic taxes, along with annual tax reports. It is critical to handle them correctly and on time, as improper tax filings could set you up for an audit, back taxes owed, and even civil or criminal penalties. Use a tax professional to handle these things, if necessary, as the cost will be offset in the end.

Business Transition Documents

Business Sale or Purchase Agreement This is the contract for the purchase or sale of a business or share.

Franchise Agreement This is the contract for the purchase or sale of franchise rights to a particular business. It may go in conjunction with the purchase or sale of an existing business or independently as the rights to start a new business.

Merger, Partnership or Other Agreement These documents deal with joining an entity or person with an existing business. The documents should not only include the current merger or acquisition agreement, but also the long-term operating agreement detailing how the business will function and look when this transaction is complete.

Liquidation Agreement This agreement is related to the liquidation or dissolution of a business. These agreements could be general or through the court system. They can also be individualized with individual consumers or creditors. It is key that these agreements address the personal liability of any business owners in addition to the business itself.

Once you recognize that managing paperwork and documentation properly is a critical part of every business, you will come to see that setting things up and maintaining order is just part of the works. Establishing the proper documents, procedures and record keeping is key to quality operations.

M.R.M.

YAY! Regulations!

*Sometimes they can save you money
and protect you from losses.*

LET'S NOT GET CARRIED AWAY, moving forward so fast that you neglect the basic regulations that apply to your business: resellers' certificates, multi-state certificates, liability insurance, Uniform Commercial Code (UCC) statutes, proper employee and/or independent contractor paperwork, etc.

You would be surprised at how many entrepreneurs haven't gone through the necessary steps to properly engage in business on a business-to-business (B2B) or business-to-consumer (B2C) level. I've been in countless meeting with first-time business owners who didn't realize that filings with various levels of government were needed to permit them to engage in commerce. These conversations are the most fun when you tell a business owner that she is actually doing much better than she originally thought, because due to her lack of a reseller certificate, she hasn't been getting credits for pass-through taxes she's paid on the component goods she purchases to make the products she sells.

Certificates and tax implications

"Oh, wow!" she says. "You mean if I get this simple certificate, then I don't have to pay tax when I buy components used to make my product?" Yes, that is correct (but check on this in your own locality). Now this new business owner wants to know how it will change her business's financials.

Well let's see: In this particular example, the client's business was based in a location where the sales tax rate was 6.5 percent. With the certificate, she no longer will be paying that 6.5 percent on components for her end products. Therefore, her cost of goods will drop 6.5 percent from where they are currently.

Goods and Services Tax, Value Added Tax

If your business is located in a country that imposes Goods and Services Tax (GST) or Value Added Tax (VAT), or something similar to them known by a different name, you should know that you can recoup some of the tax that was applied to the goods and services your business buys. In turn, you charge VAT or GST for things you sell, and the balance between the two will lead to a refund or payment due, depending on your current period's numbers.

Liabilities

As we have seen, another gap in some starters' knowledge concerns liability insurance, covering both your products and services. You just never know what can go wrong, even if you have the best intentions. You wouldn't want to own a small landscape company and happen to shoot a rock through the customer's high-end, energy-saving glass in an exotic set of French doors. That fix could cost you more than you billed for the job. Equally, you wouldn't want to own an auto repair shop and accidentally install something wrong that causes a car accident or bodily harm. Mistakes like this happen every day. They can lead to lawsuits and in turn settlements that can leave business owners and their businesses wiped out financially. It's just not worth avoiding some of the little steps that can protect you, your business and your family.

Uniform Commercial Code (UCC)

Understanding and complying with UCC regulations are critical for doing business in the United States. Most starters don't understand that there are certain regulations that affect B2B dealings and that other regulations exist to protect consumers in B2C transactions.

In my opinion, one of the most important UCC regulations has to do with implied warranties in B2C transactions. Many entrepreneurs get hung up on the idea that they need to check the expressed warranties of products they buy for their businesses with competing products' warranties. Some people even fall for the warranty gimmicks that are presented by most of the "big box" stores regarding additional service and protection plans. These can be a waste of money. In a *Consumer Reports* study it was found that only 42 percent (not even half of extended warranties, such as protection plans) were even used.

Sure, it's great to know that you can simply bring a product back to a store and it will be replaced on the spot. However, what did you pay for that privilege? Often the upcharge incurred at the time of purchase is 20 to 30 percent of the original purchase price!

What most people don't understand is that all consumer goods are forced by Article 2, Section 315 of the UCC regulations to carry implied warranties relating to merchantability for professional merchants and warranty of fitness for all sellers. These simply mean that the product being sold has to do what it is built to do, address the buyer's need and it must perform to a level that is expected by the buyer. If the product fails to fulfill these basic characteristics then it is in violation of the UCC regulations.

Employee-related regulations

Lastly, make sure you know what regulations apply for you to properly document the types of employees and independent contractors who work with you or for you. Now, more than ever, it is important to cross every "t" and dot every "i" in employment papers; otherwise you may find yourself in a heap of trouble. Make sure never to refer to independent contractors as employees in any correspondence. Also, if you have employees that you are in the process of reclassifying as independent contractors, get legal advice before you proceed. There are strict regulations in most places regarding these actions, and you'll want to follow them scrupulously.

M.O.

Using Contracts on the Regular

Make life simpler with contract templates.

AHHH, CONTRACTS.... Contracts may seem like tedious, stiffly written documents to non-legal people, but they do tend to make everyone feel secure once the signing parties have hammered out the terms. Sadly, however, not all contracts are examples of excellent work. It is common for contracts to be riddled with loopholes, carve-outs and exceptions. And sometimes they lack enforceability when they are put to the test. So it pays to make sure every contract you have is clear, correct, and complete.

Have a frank discussion with your attorney about how much contract work each of you should do, given the different circumstances that arise in your business. Begin by identifying the contracts you use frequently and set them up as templates that properly trained and authorized people can execute on behalf of your business. That leaves contracts that are not routine to be worked up by your attorney.

When things go wrong

A well-written contract anticipates the kinds of problems that can happen and sets up pre-agreed ways to handle them: non-delivery, late payment, sharing information that's confidential or proprietary, and many other things. Sometimes, though, unexpected things occur and there's no guidance in the contract. Or sometimes, the other party breaches the terms agreed to (meaning that the party breaks one or more of the "rules" in the contract) and refuses to or is unable to remedy the situation. Rarely, the other party signs the contract in bad faith and conducts business in ways that the contract prohibits.

Unfortunately, often you will find that it is too costly to pursue damages from a party that has breached a contract and refuses to remedy it. If the amount due you is fairly small, you may be able to take it to a small claims court, represent yourself, and produce documents and details to support your case (check out this option in your own locality). However, most businesses that seek damages from a breach of contract are looking for an amount that involves lawyers and costs hefty fees. I've seen businesses go bankrupt because of the legal fees they've incurred seeking damages from one breach.

There's another problem, too: When a breach of contact has taken place, it is often harder than you would think to prove it. Most agreement violations are not black and white; they sit somewhere in a gray zone. Then it ends up being one individual's word against another's, with a few ambiguously written texts and emails supporting each party's argument.

Depending on the situation, if you can find a way to resolve the issues through negotiation and perhaps compromise, you will save legal fees, time and frustration. So give that approach your best effort if you have that option.

With all that said, I always use contracts to record the parties' agreement. Having contacts in place, whether it be with investors, lenders, employees, third party contractors, professional resources, suppliers, landlords, public utilities, and so forth, makes life much simpler and frees people to do the work they expect to do.

So it's *always* best to make the effort to document important agreements. This way no one is confused by the roles and responsibilities of others. Confusion happens more often than you would think. Most people have the best intentions of following through to the best of their ability in regard to whatever event or agreement is being managed by a contact. However each person may have a different interpretation of what to do, how to do it, how much time it should take, how much commitment has been made, what is expected of them, and what they expect of others.

Clarity is not always hard—the joys of templates

This is why I prefer to use contacts that are written in very clear and concise language that specifies who is involved, the roles and responsibilities of both parties, timetables, milestones, deadlines, costs, contributions, considerations offered by both, terms, termination information and more. Luckily most of the language that an entrepreneur or business owner wants to place in a contract can be used over and over again, as long as it pertains to the same type of contract or agreement.

For example, an employment agreement may prohibit disclosure of business information and trade secrets. The same document may discuss what is expected of every employee, regardless of position, and it may detail the processes and protocols for communicating on behalf of the company. These types of things can be drafted once and used over and over again, making it easy to issue new employment agreements as your team grows.

Whether you produce goods or services, your attorney can create standardized contract language to articulate the way payment processes are handled: how your business expects to be paid, when you issue invoices, your payment terms, types of payments accepted, how credits are handled, point-of-contact for receivables and other necessary disclosures. With a little thought you can come up with a list of template needs and guidelines for issuing them.

A real-life example

When Scott Girard and I were manufacturing electromechanical products in southeast Asia, we learned the value of having our payment terms spelled out. A large, longstanding U.S. client asked us to re-engineer a few designs and show them different variants of the product. They wanted to see everything as soon as possible. At the time our sourcing and manufacturing business was still in its infancy, and we knew rush service would cost a lot. Happily, we put an agreement in place that required our client to reimburse us for all sampling, shipping and logistic expenses at the time of delivery. Then, in the event that they moved forward with a large order, we would credit them the amount previously collected. That practice, and that template agreement, became standard for us.

In this way we avoided costly cash flow issues and gained the ability to service multiple clients without having to worry about incurring horrendous up-front expenses. It also encouraged our clients to follow through with orders, because they would get a credit. To us, even as a small start-up, it was worth crediting substantial sums we'd spent on engineering, sampling and air freighting, once we won the business.

One time, after we delivered a batch of rush samples, we politely produced an invoice for the preparation expenses. The project manager freaked. Once he regained his composure, he realized that he hadn't authorized the work, but his recently retired subordinate had, on behalf of the company. He asked us to work it out with the new subordinate. That person started to refuse to pay. We explained that we had an agreement and produced the signed copy of the agreement that was put in place by her predecessor. We were soon handed a check and off we went.

The moral? Protect yourself with contracts!

M.O.

The Who-What-When-Why-How of Contracts

*It's remarkable what a few pieces of paper
can do for—or against—a business.*

CONTRACTS HAVE A WAY OF INTIMIDATING, frustrating or even boring some entrepreneurs. We propose to present a cram course in contracts in the next few sections, with no final exam involved. In fact, you could read through to see what's included, then come back to focus on things you need to know or do when the need arises. To get started, here are the fundamentals of business contracts and some tips about common-sense contract habits.

Who? As we've said, you and/or your business (depending on its structure) should contract with every person, entity and organization that your business depends on. Yes, it takes extra time, but I assure you that it will save you time and money in the end by clearly defining the expectations of all parties. Unfortunately, most entrepreneurs learn this lesson from the school of hard knocks. Insisting on a contract will add credibility to your business transactions. Do you think Fortune 500 companies do business on a handshake?

What? A written document signed by all parties, in accordance with all local laws, that both parties understand and including all the key elements we will discuss in the next section. Each party should get a copy of the fully signed contract. These do not all need to be unique forms; there are many templates and standard forms available. You can customize your own standard forms for various aspects of your business, for example a standard lease, a standard sales contract or a standard purchasing order. Your attorney may even construct interchangeable clauses to use as needed, like a template library that lets you create your own contracts.

When? All the time, every time. Consider it a safety net under the high wire. Once a contract is in place, it should not affect your ongoing operations, but it should always be there just in case you need it. When in doubt, contract it.

Why? Contracts manage the expectations of all parties. They define their roles, responsibilities and obligations. Contracts provide mutual assurances and remedies to all parties in the event of a breach. They lend credibility to your business operation and maintain fair dealing. And often, the discussion and negotiation that leads up to a signing can a very productive, relationship-building exercise.

How? Make contracting a condition of doing business. Use templates and pre-drafted clauses for efficiency and cost savings. Call your business attorney whenever you aren't sure if your archive or some special assistance works best.

General tips for business contracting

- Write it out. Put all contracts in writing.

- Keep it simple. Yes, contracting can be complicated, but your contract does not need to be. Keep it as simple as possible to communicate what is needed.

- Deal with decision makers. Contract negotiations often get bogged down as proposals are passed around teams or committees. Make sure you are negotiating directly with the person who has the power to make the decision, cutting out as many middle people as possible.

- Identify parties properly. Make sure you understand who is who in a contract and what the obligations, remedies and defenses of each party are.

- Specify payment information. Business is all about money. Therefore, when it comes to money in your contract, you must be as specific as possible. "Payment each calendar month" does not specify the amount or a day of the month. Both could be significant to a small business.

- Default or breach. Define what each of these are under your contract. Be clear about what is a big deal to you and what your expectations are.

- Remedies. You should clearly define what how the other party should fix the situation if they do default or breach the contract.

- Termination clause. Define how or when this contract ends and what you expect to happen then.

- Dispute resolution. Specify how you want to work out disputes. Yes, they *will* happen. Do you want to require mediation or arbitration? Do you want a prevailing parties' clause? That ensures that the loser of the case pays the winner's attorney fees if you are forced to go to court.

- Governing law. What law or rules control the contract? Is there a specific court that should hear disputes? Is this jurisdiction beneficial to you?

- Confidentiality. Are the contents of this contract confidential? Is it public information? Is there any potential harm if others see the terms of this contract? Is this properly addressed in the contract?

- Practicalities. Sign in blue ink so originals are easily identified. Always add a date when you sign or initial a document. If you are signing for the company, add your title. Initial and date any hand-written changes in a printed document (and do likewise at the bottom of each page to ensure a signed document contains all the correct, final pages). Fill in or strike through every blank in the contract so there's no confusion later. Note in the contract who is keeping the original(s). Make sure to record the contract if that is required. Create a single "Calendry" document that records all significant milestone dates for all your important contracts: renewals, expirations, payment dates, etc., and install the dates on your company's server or shared drive so it is accessible to anybody who needs to act on the information. Create reminders that pop up *before* the milestone date to give you time to prepare and complete the action on time.

Memorandum of Understanding (MOU), Memorandum of Agreement (MOA)

A Memorandum of Understanding (MOU) is a legal document, but it is usually not binding. That means that if one party does not comply or if they breach the understanding, then there are most likely no penalties or remedies for the breach. Think of an MOU as a "contract light."

MOUs have two primary purposes. The first is as the initial step in formal contract negotiations. Many complex contracts require significant time and resources to research, create and execute. In such cases, you can draw up an MOU to set the conditions, specifications and limitations of the contract's purpose and then proceed with the negotiation. For example, if you make widgets, you can sign a MOU with a supplier, stating that you will order a minimum quantity of a particular component (perhaps with pricing and delivery terms or targets), if the supplier can produce them. Therefore your supplier is protected and incentivized to conduct the research to determine whether he is able to supply that component as specified.

The second purpose is as a non-binding statement of intention. This is most often used by governmental agencies or for the purposes of public policy. For example, nations may execute MOUs related to weaponry that do not meet the formal requirements of a treaty, or governmental agencies may use MOUs to set the general knowledge of programs or facts. In the private sector, MOUs are often used in relation to public policy. For example, major clothing companies may sign a MOU stating they will ensure specified minimum working conditions in outsourced factories.

MOUs are rare in small and startup businesses. In their place, entrepreneurs sometimes use Memoranda of Agreement (MOAs). These may be binding or non-binding, but they are better than handshakes in pinning down what two parties are trying to achieve together, particularly if the goal requires good-faith actions before the full deal can be formalized. MOAs typically describe how two parties plan to work together on a defined project. (Picture an MOA saying you'll provide your customer with three designs and pricing for a wedding dress, for which she'll pay you a design fee, and then she will pick one design, you will make that dress, and she will buy it.).

MOUs and MOAs vary substantially by document type and jurisdiction, so even if they are non-binding, you must carefully review each one before signing. Do not assume that the document has one meaning or is non-binding simply because it's called an MOU or MOA. As we've repeatedly said, it never hurts to check with your attorney if you have any questions or doubts.

Contracts are the asphalt on the superhighways of commerce. They are truly where the rubber meets the road, and are critically important in managing the risk and expectations of business relationships. A savvy businessperson uses contracts as a fundamental tool for achieving business success.

M.R.M.

The Pen is Mightier than the Sword

When in doubt, write it out

A CONTRACT IS A LAWFUL AGREEMENT. *Lawful* means something recognized by law, meaning you can enforce its terms through the legal system.

Contracts can be oral, written or implied. They can be between two parties; among many parties, groups or entities; and any combination thereof—that's why we use the word *party* to refer to a participant in a contract, because it may not be a human being. Contracts can be renewed (or left to expire without renewal), terminated, broken, set aside (in some cases), or remedied and enforced (in others). They are crucial in business because they ensure that each party has a clear understanding of what to expect from the other, both in good times and bad.

In this section we will take a look at the essential elements of a contract and how the parties agree to perform. In the following section we'll take up contract enforcement.

Elements of a contract

To be valid, a contract must have certain parts. These parts may vary slightly between different jurisdictions, but the basics are Offer, Acceptance, Meeting of the Minds, Promise to Perform in Return for Valuable Consideration, and finally definitions of a Specific Time, plus Specific Conditions and Performance.

The first part, the **Offer**, is a promise to do or not to do something, in exchange for something. Either party in a contract can make the offer or counteroffer. Examples include a landlord who offers to provide a commercial space, a supplier who offers to supply components of a certain specification, a professional who offers not to disclose confidential information, a delivery company who offers to deliver certain items at a certain time, or a buyer who offers to purchase a certain number of products at a certain time and price. Offers must be specific in their terms and communicated to the other party. They may be terminated or revoked by the party making the offer.

Next comes the **Acceptance**. The other party must do something (communicate, sign, pay, etc.) to "manifest assent" i.e., accept the offer. And the accepting party must accept the offer exactly. Any negotiation or counter offers mean that you have not actually accepted the offer. This is called the "mirror image rule". The rule states that to accept the offer, you must accept the exact "mirror image" of the offer made by the offering party. In the previous examples, acceptance happens when the tenant signs the lease, the manufacturer signs a letter of intent, the professional signs and begins a consultation, the receiving company pays or the selling company notifies the buyer of shipment.

The next part is the **Meeting of the Minds**. This is the requirement that all parties have the same understanding of the contract terms and that all parties intend to be bound by the contract. Reaching a meeting of the minds can be more difficult than you might expect. For example, if a party contacts a business and offers to buy all of the "stock", the other party could assume the word "stock" to mean: (1) the shares of the business, (2) the inventory of goods on hand, or even (3) the cattle owned by the business. That's because "stock" has multiple meanings. So when in doubt, specify and double check. Contract law is full of disputes where reasonable people understand the meaning of words in greatly different ways.

The **Promise to Perform in Return for Valuable Consideration** is the next requirement in most contracts. This happens in a bilateral contract, where both parties give something up. Most jurisdictions require that a contract be bilateral for the contract to be enforceable. The majority of contracts used in business are, and should be, bilateral. Compare them to a unilateral contract, where only one party promises to do something. (Picture offering a reward for a lost item: You oblige yourself to pay, but no other party is required to act.) "Valuable consideration" means that both parties have skin in the game. There is no specific value that must be included in a contract for it to count as valuable. Consideration can take the form of an act, a specific non-act, a product or money.

Finally, specific terms such as **Time, Specifications and Conditions** must be included in the contract. These terms will vary significantly by jurisdiction and industry. Again, the goal is to clearly define what each side must do as part of the contract and set the expectations of all parties.

Performance

Now that the contract is fully formed, there must be the performance of the contract obligations. Performance can be considered actual, attempted or partial, or non-performance. Contrary to what you might think from talking to most attorneys, all parties actually satisfactorily perform in the overwhelming majority of contracts.

Actual performance is doing what you are supposed to do under the contract. The contract will then be completed, or remain in ongoing good standing, based on the type of contract it is. **Attempted or partial performance** happens when a party makes best efforts but does not complete the process; unforeseen changes to either party or process occur while executing a contract; or a party performs the majority of obligations under the contract, but not everything. Examples include delivering goods that the purchaser no longer needs and will not accept; interference by natural disasters such as hurricanes; or building a complete office building, but putting a roof on it that is different from what the contract required. Each of these situations needs to be addressed in the contract, along with **non-performance or breach**, in the situation where a party does not or cannot fulfill its commitments.

With what you now know about contracts, and guidance as needed from your attorney, you can use these powerful tools to help shape your business's future. But read on, because sometimes the troubleshooting clauses of a contract suddenly come into play.

M.R.M

When the Wheels Come Off ...

Contracts really can protect your business interests.

IT'S IMPORTANT TO REMEMBER on some days that contracts are intended to keep things running smoothly. Unfortunately, you and those you deal with will encounter occasions where things don't go as planned, and while the contract is in place, you still hit unwelcome road bumps. Forewarned is forearmed, as they say.

Breach of contract

A breach of contract occurs when one party does not do what it is supposed to do under the contract. As we saw above, this could be attempted, partial performance or non-performance of the contract—all of these could be deemed a breach of contract. The categories of breach are material, fundamental, minor and anticipatory.

A **material** breach is a very serious breach that goes to the heart of the contract, undermines the agreement as a whole and gives the non-breaching party the right to sue. For example, a supplier delivers a shipment of green socks but the contract specifies that the purchaser needs white shirts. A breach of contract has occurred. The purchaser has been damaged. But the supplier may be able to partially perform the contract obligations by delivering the white shirts overnight.

A **fundamental** breach is also a very serious breach, one that gives the non-breaching party the right to immediately terminate the contract and sue. Unlike a material breach, a fundamental breach makes any performance of the contract impossible. For example, you contract with a landlord to lease a site for your business, but when you arrive to move in, there is another business operating in that site with a valid lease. Since there would most likely be no way for the landlord to perform under the contract, you could terminate immediately and sue. This is the type of breach that most often ends up in court.

A **minor breach** is partial performance of the contract. The issues do not go to the heart of the contract and the non-breaching party is not allowed to terminate the entire contract, but is allowed to sue for damages. For example, you contract with a builder to build you an office building with a red roof. The builder produces a building that meets all specifications except it has a blue roof. Unless specifically identified in the contract, this would be a minor breach, and the builder could only be liable for the cost to correct the roof. You would not be able to cancel the entire contract.

An **anticipatory breach or anticipatory repudiation** is a breach that occurs when one party, through words or actions, notifies the other party that it will not meet its obligations under the contract. This occurs prior to the actual contract deadline and gives the non-breaching party the option of renegotiating or terminating the contract. These breaches can be of all levels of severity. Examples include a contract to landscape your factory's entry area on a specific day. The landscaper calls to say that his equipment is broken and that he will be unable to landscape your property for an additional two weeks. Or suppose you sign a commercial lease contract for space in a building to be built and finished by a certain date. But construction has not started ten days before your move-in date, and it obviously will be impossible to complete the construction in time.

Damages and equitable relief? A question of money or no money.

If a party does breach a contract, how do you fix it? You go for a remedy. Remedies describe the options available to a party when there is a breach of a contract. The non-breaching party may use these remedies to fix the breach or at least to try and make it better. There are two broad categories of remedies: damages and equitable relief. Let's look at each in turn.

Damages equal money. Depending on the type of breach, the non-breaching party may be automatically entitled to or have the right to seek various types of monetary solutions. These could be specified by your contract or jurisdiction, or they could also be industry specific. The party seeking damages may be required to prove the exact amount needed to remedy the breach, or the amount could be specified by contract. The types of damages available are compensatory damages, consequential and incidental damages, liquidated damages, punitive damages or attorney's fees.

Compensatory damages are also known as actual damages. They are paid to compensate a party for actual known losses. These monetary losses are a direct result of the breach of contract. They are designed to make the non-breaching party whole again or to restore it to the way it was prior to the breach. Common examples of compensatory damages are payment of lost wages and medical bills for an employee injured on the job, or the actual loss of value to property because the contracted act did not occur.

Consequential and incidental damages are also known as special damages. They are paid to compensate a party for losses indirectly caused by the breach and that are reasonably foreseeable, based on the circumstances. Common examples are payment for temporary office space and storage if a leased office is not available on the contracted move-in date, or an amount paid to hire extra laborers, when a moving company fails to provide the number of personnel required under a contract.

Liquidated damages are also known as ascertained damages. They are specific damage amounts written into the contract and agreed to by the parties as part of the contracting process. The purpose is to compensate the non-breaching party for losses incurred, *not* to punish either party. Liquidated damage amounts must be reasonable when compared to the actual damage for the breach. Generally, this type of damage is used when the estimated possible damages at the time of contracting are unknown and the parties want to save time in calculating damages if a breach occurs. Common examples of liquidated damages are late fees on credit card accounts, or the loss of a deposit if a buyer fails to close the purchase of a property by a certain date.

Punitive damages are also known as exemplary damages. They are used to punish or make an example out of the breaching party. Punitive damages are awarded in addition to other types of damages and their amount and application are set by local statute. Generally, punitive damages are not available in contract matters, unless there is intentional wrongdoing or gross negligence. Common examples of punitive damages would include damages against Ponzi scams, as they not only breach the contract but also intentionally defraud the consumer. Another example would be a transportation company dispatching a driver known to be intoxicated. This would most likely constitute gross negligence.

The final category of damages is **attorneys' fees and costs**, also known as a prevailing party clause. It must be noted that many jurisdictions follow the "American Rule", which states each party is responsible for its own legal expenses unless specified by contract or statute. These types of damages are designed to cover expenses arising from the breach by one party. Attorneys' fees clauses are common in real estate contracts. Any time this clause in used in a contract, you must pay special attention to the language used, as it can be very difficult to define which is the "prevailing" party. Common examples of court costs by statute are consumer protection laws that award attorney's fees for breaches by debt collectors.

Equitable relief

Equitable relief means NO money. Equitable remedies are related to actions and fairness. These remedies are generally only available when damages (i.e., money) is insufficient to make the non-breaching party whole again. Courts strongly prefer monetary remedies over equitable remedies, as equitable remedies often require the ongoing supervision of the court. Equitable relief may be used in conjunction with monetary damages, i.e., you can receive both, and you can have multiple types of each in the same matter. The primary types of equitable relief available in contract law are specific performance, injunction, rescission and reformation.

Specific performance is an order from the court to a party to take a certain action or to perform a specific act as directed in the contract. The court orders a party to do what it was supposed to do under the contract. This type of remedy is used primarily in transactional contracts where the subject property is unique. Common examples are real estate, custom vehicles and distinctive jewelry transactions. Specific performance is not used in many types of contract disputes, such as employment contracts, due to the supervision requirement and subjective nature of actual performance. For example, a court would not order a breaching builder to specifically build you a factory.

Injunction is the exact opposite of specific performance. An injunction is an order from the court to *not* take a certain action or to *not* perform a specific act. The court orders a party not to do something related to the contract or the parties involved in the contract. Violations of an injunctive order can result in civil and even criminal penalties. Common contract-related examples include the prevention of the wrongful transfer of property, patent infringement, trade secret disclosure, tortious interference in contracts and ongoing defamation.

Rescission is an equitable remedy that unmakes or sets aside the contract so that both parties return to their original pre-contract positions. Some jurisdictions refer to this as canceling or reversing a contract. Rescission may be completed by a single party, if it is allowed under the contract, by multiple parties through mutual consent, or by the court; although court action is very rare with privately negotiated contracts. For rescission to be an available option, the parties must be able to return to their pre-contract positions and the rescission must not inhibit the rights of a non-party obtained through the contract. A common example would be a contract cancelation that is permitted if done in an initial grace period.

Reformation, also known as rectification of a contract, is re-writing the contract to clarify the original intent of the parties and to correct mistakes or misrepresentations. The parties may reform a contract at any time through mutual agreement. However, most parties will do this through modification or addendum rather than reforming the original contract. Courts can also reform contracts, but prefer not to. Most courts will only pursue reformation if the contract was valid, the breach will be remedied by the reformation and there are no other defenses are available. A typical example of reformation is the rewriting of a real estate contract to correct an incorrect property address.

Contract defenses

In addition to the remedies available for a breach we have just reviewed, there are also a number of defenses available to challenge the breach or even to challenge the contract itself. These defenses could mitigate the breach or cause the contract to be void, voidable or unenforceable. *Void* means it is as if the contract was never formed. *Voidable* means that at least one party can cancel the contract. *Unenforceable* means that neither party may enforce the other's obligations. Here are some of the most common contract defenses.

Form of Contract Certain types of contracts, such as real estate, must be in writing to be enforceable; thus an oral real estate contract could easily be challenged as unenforceable.

Fraud or Misrepresentation A contract is voidable if a party was induced to enter the contract through false statements or omissions of material facts.

Undue Influence or Duress A contract is void when a party induces or coerces another party to enter the contract through exploitation of a vulnerability, a special relationship, a position of power, blackmail, extortion or direct threats.

Capacity A contract is voidable if a party lacks capacity to enter into the contract. Individuals may lack capacity due to age (being a minor), mental disabilities (Downs Syndrome, I.Q. under 70), mental incapacity (dementia) or temporary incapacity (intoxication).

Mistake A contract may be void or voidable depending on whether the mistake was only made by one party (unilateral mistake) or both parties (mutual mistake), and whether the mistake is fundamental to the purpose of the contract (common mistake).

Unconscionable A contract is voidable if it is extremely unfair and apparent from the terms of the contract that one party took advantage of the other due to an imbalance of bargaining power or exploitation of low education.

Illegal or Public Policy A contract is void if performance under the contract by either party violates the law, is based on an illegal purpose or is otherwise incompatible with public policy.

Frustration of Purpose or Impossibility A contract is unenforceable if there is no longer a valid purpose for the contract or if performance becomes impossible.

Now that you know more than you ever wanted to know about the inner and outer workings of contracts, you'll really be able to work productively with your business attorney. Who knows? Maybe you'll find it so fascinating that you decide to chuck your business and go to law school!

M.R.M.

Here's a Loan, There's a Loan, Everywhere's a Business Loan!

*If you're not quite conversant with legalese,
a lawyer can be a great translator!*

Whether you need a business loan for real estate, start-up capital, operating capital, equipment, etc., the process is never as easy as you think. And with the large sums of money typically involved with a business loan, the last thing you want is to not use it wisely or to accidentally default because you didn't understand the terms. Even successful small businesses that are turning a profit often get into financial trouble because the owner didn't fully understand the terms of her business loan.

Most commonly, the business owner thinks that she will have a few years before she has to start paying the loan back (which is sometimes true with business loans). So she uses her loan to buy real estate or a bunch of equipment and supplies. Then she finds out that her first loan payment is due at the beginning of the very next month! Impossible? It happens all the time. This is just a simple example, but the point is this: Commercial loan terms are extremely complicated. Not necessarily because the lender is deliberately trying to be confusing or deceptive; it's just the way is.

It's true, loans are complicated, but with due diligence or proper advice from an attorney, they are nothing to fear. You may also find that the complexity of a loan is directly tied to the "customizability" of your loan. If you plan right and know what you need, you can probably get a loan to fit. For example, do you just need to buy time, and then your business will explode? Then how about a loan with no payments due for five years, with the entire amount is due in Year Six? That formula, calling for a balloon payment, is just one option. But you need to know what you need.

Indeed, the most common cause of business failure related to commercial loans is poor planning, specifically: not borrowing enough money, and neglecting to budget for the loan's repayment over its term.

How much should I borrow?

Let's suppose you need start-up money. The amount you borrow should be calculated to cover critical costs and salaries. You need to pay not only the immediate costs you are borrowing for, but also to sustain the business until it reaches the breakeven point in your business plan. Most borrowers focus on only the immediate cost and naturally try to minimize the amount they borrow. For example, if they are purchasing a new brick and mortar location, they will total up the purchase prices and immediate transactions costs, but often forget to include the costs of moving, remodeling, advertising to promote the new location, increased labor costs, likely employee turnover, insurance, loss of revenue during the move, etc.

They also fail to add in money to ensure the business owner and all employees are paid. A safety net must be built into all financial calculations to ensure all get paid (and yes, that includes the business owner). A missed paycheck can quickly turn an employee into a former employee, and after that, your next lawsuit. You need to take care of yourself too. Lack of income to a business owner can lead to self-doubt, demotivation and family problems.

The other expense new entrepreneurs often fail to consider and budget for is the loan repayment, as we saw above. Even though it's obvious that you must repay your loan, entrepreneurs often just overlook the terms, especially for loans that defer the initial payment (i.e., no payments for Year One). Or they don't plan for loans with escalator clauses (e.g., Year One = X per month, Year Two = X + 2, Year Three = X +3, etc.). I have seen many businesses in trouble because they failed to plan for the payments due on the loan.

These issues can be a slippery slope that takes a business from expansion to termination very quickly. Consider them very carefully when deciding how much to borrow.

Keep in mind that large lending institutions issue many loans every day, so even though the process is complicated, their people do it all the time. A new business owner may be a hot shot in his industry, but that doesn't mean he can keep up with the big-dog lenders when it comes to comprehending the ins-and-outs of a loan contract. The commercial loan application process also can be very tricky and large sums of money can be at stake. (When you apply for a commercial loan, collateral of real property is typically required, which makes the stakes even more serious.)

A key distinction lenders make is whether the business has "independent" or "stand alone" credit. Does the business have its own credit score already? Then it stands alone. If so, then the business can sign the loan and also possibly put up collateral. If the business does not have stand-alone credit, then the lender will most likely want at least one of the owners to "put skin in the game" by either personally guaranteeing or pledging personal collateral to the lender.

Lenders are in the business of making money at zero risk to themselves. The loan contract will be airtight for them, and they can afford very good lawyers to ensure they maintain their zero-risk status. This may or may not be at your expense. Again, this is not because they're nasty people; it is simply because they are in the zero-risk loan business.

Bring that lawyer in!

Regrettably, a large number of potential entrepreneurs are scared away from starting a business altogether because the business loan process can be so intimidating. They know they are out-gunned in the knowledge department, but for some reason think that a commercial attorney will not be any help. Let me lay it out for you: I would *never* go into a commercial lender's office without a business lawyer. Ever. If you were taking out a loan for a million dollars and were on the hook to pay it back, wouldn't you want to know if the terms of the loan were fair and legal? This is just one of those cost-benefit scenarios, where the small cost on the front end pays off dividends for the life of your business.

Even if you get a loan, you're apt to have questions. If a lender doesn't have the best staff in place, sometimes it can even be hard for non-finance-based entrepreneurs to ask the lender questions about their loan, and understand the answers they get in return. A commercial lawyer can help translate and explain to you in common terms what your lender's answers mean. You could spend four hours Googling every single word in your contract that you don't know and still not really know what you are about to promise. (But what entrepreneur has time for that? If you do, then I want a copy of your business plan!) Or you can pay a business lawyer for an hour of his time to tell you everything you want to know and warn you about things you never suspected.

In that regard, it is extremely important to remember what incentives are motivating the various parties and professionals involved. Specifically, lenders, bankers and loan offices are paid, usually by a substantial commission, when a loan is funded or finalized. Therefore they are motivated to make the loan happen, not to look out for your best interests. Similarly, closing agents, real estate and business brokers are paid when the transaction closes and are therefore primarily motivated to close the transaction. Your attorney is paid to look out for your interests regardless of what happens in the transaction, and is incentivized to give you good advice and keep you as a client. Your attorney may be the only person who is fully on your team.

Hard times?

So now let's assume you've secured your commercial loan (with or without a business lawyer) and fall on hard times. Unfortunately, you still owe more on your commercial loan than you can afford to pay. Not the best situation, I agree, but it happens.

In the event of default, you'll need professional protection to help you work through the problem. You think the tax collectors can get ugly? Try defaulting on a commercial loan. You probably won't find a horse's head in your bed, but it still won't be a pleasant experience, and let's not even mention your credit score.

You'll surely need a lawyer to help you negotiate debt settlement if you default on a commercial loan. Beyond helping you pay the lowest possible amount to settle your debt with the commercial lender, in some cases, debt settlement can help free up cash flows to possibly save your struggling business.

It's true! Sometimes when businesses are in a situation where they can still turn a small profit, but can't pay all their employees *and* make their commercial loan payment, a commercial attorney can work some "lawyer magic" and strike a sweet deal with the lender to lower or postpone payments. How can they do that? Because they know how! The lender is even more likely to listen to a commercial attorney than a tearful, terrified, struggling entrepreneur because the attorney is businesslike. The lender doesn't have a problem with taking over an entrepreneur's house or her kids' college funds. It's just business. And sometimes seizing personal assets pledged as collateral is part of a risk-averse business.

So here's the bottom line: If you let a commercial lawyer help you through the loan application and management process, you have a better chance of securing it and operating within the structure of that loan. If you default on the loan, you have a much better chance of saving the business with a lawyer in your corner. It would be a terrible waste of a great business idea if you defaulted on a business loan by accident!

S.G. and M.R.M.

CHAPTER IV

Growth and Exit Activities

Using a Corporate Attorney to Ward Off Trouble

It's smart to have a business lawyer handy to help keep you out of trouble, not get out of trouble.

THE BIGGEST AND MOST OBVIOUS reason for working with a business lawyer is to keep your business on the right side of the law *before* something bad happens. One accidental wrong move can put your whole business at risk.

Say you open a business selling unique handmade jewelry. You go the safe route and start small, renting booths at local craft fairs and flea markets, and soon your jewelry is just flying off your table. You really can't make it fast enough. Before long, you've incorporated yourself, quit your day job, built a website, purchased a van, hit the road, and you're marketing your jewelry to every small boutique in the region!

Unfortunately, you didn't do adequate market research before starting up. When you get to a small, quaint local jewelry shop in a distant town, you see a necklace and earrings hanging in the shop window that look remarkably similar to your design. When you ask the clerk about the items and show her yours, she informs you that not only is she the shop owner, she's also the jeweler who made them, and she legally protected her design when she created it… 15 years ago!

Oh, and by the way, she has a business lawyer. He quickly sends a cease and desist letter to your official corporate address. The letter says something like this, translated from legalese: *Stop making and selling your jewelry that looks just like my design-protected jewelry, or I'm going to sue the pants off you!*

Business lawyers can help you do the necessary research, right from the start, to ensure you don't get blind-sided. They can also help you manage all kinds of other problems. Consider these what-if's.

1.   What if a customer gets hurt or killed using your product?

2.   What if someone tries to sue you for any reason?

3.   What if a delivery person falls and gets a concussion in your office?

4.   What if someone tries to rob you at gunpoint in your shop?

5.   What if a customer or employee steals from you?

6.   What if a customer breaks a very expensive product, then refuses to pay for it, and your insurance won't cover the loss?

7.   What if an employee shows up to work drunk, falls off a ladder, and breaks a hip?

8.   What if a problem employee, the one who didn't get the promotion he wanted, responds by claiming that you sexually harassed him?

9.   What if one of your employees commits a hit-and-run accident in one of your company vehicles?

10.   What if your corporate accountant forgets to pay your business's taxes for a decade?

The answer to every single one of these questions should be overwhelmingly obvious: *I'm going to call my attorney!*

An attorney can help you understand the specific legal issues surrounding your business or field. Say you're a magician. It doesn't matter if you're selling out casinos in Las Vegas or selling out sandboxes at children's birthday parties. According to a U.S. law from 1970, you must have a "disaster plan" for your rabbit. I'm not joking. This disaster plan must cover fires, floods, tornadoes, snowstorms, power failures, fleas, and poisoned carrots. (Okay, I might have made that last one up.) Seriously though, if you're a magician, you must keep a strict travel itinerary for your furry sidekick when you take him out of town and be open to random inspections by the United States Department of Agriculture (USDA). Of course, there is also an annual fee of $40 to keep your magic rabbit licensed.

Corporate attorneys provide broad-based, long-term business advice on typically complicated matters. This often starts with helping you structure your business the right way. They can help you with support on matters ranging from incorporating your new business, to opening your doors, to growing it, right through to selling or closing your business.

I know a local business owner who took a do-it-yourself approach and paid the price. He intended to start his business small, grow it, and eventually sell shares to the public by making an Initial Public Offering (IPO). He did a ton of research, achieved all of his growth targets along the way, and then started planning to take his business public. His plans came to a screeching halt, however, when he discovered that his business could not be taken public at all: It was structured and founded as a limited liability company (LLC). He had initially incorporated his business as an LLC because it was the easiest to do and the tax picture was favorable. Unfortunately, he found out the hard way that he would have to re-structure as a corporation, which would mean a new tax structure, and which ultimately meant he didn't have enough money to take his company public at that time.

If you share your long-term goals with your corporate attorney, she can assist you in making wise, long-term decisions that still meet your short-term needs. She can help you to achieve your long-term goals in a rational, efficient and legal fashion. She can keep you from having to back-pedal, side-step, shimmy, squeeze, bend, tussle or be tempted to evade the law. Obviously the best way to grow a business is to avoid doing something illegal or strategically off-course.

Business lawyers are there first of all to keep you out of trouble, as well as to help get you out of trouble. If you know when to seek good advice from your business attorney, she can keep you from making the wrong choices and winding up in the court room, or worse!

S.G.

Checking Out for Departure

Think of it as tidying up in advance.

I'M AFRAID I HAVE BAD NEWS, FRIENDS. You're going to die. In fact, we are *all* going to die. To make matters worse, most of us have no idea when it will happen. The only sure thing is that we will.

Now that we've faced this tragic truth together, let's move on and do what we, as entrepreneurs, do best. Plan for it! Draw up a business estate plan!

Business estate plans

Business estate planning is smart, especially if you want to pass your business or stake in a business to your partners or family members. Think of a business estate plan as a living will for your business interests (your "estate"): a directive detailing how you want to dispose of them at the end of your life.

A business estate plan can accomplish two goals:

- Reduce or eliminate uncertainties that may lead to costly legal battles between partners, family members, or stakeholders

- Strategically plan to maximize the benefits to the deceased's estate while simultaneously creating or maintaining value in the business

While private individuals typically work with family law attorneys to arrange personal estate plans, you would be best served to see your corporate attorney to set up and manage your business estate plan and to integrate it properly with your personal plan. It's a business matter, and she is best prepared to establish your trust.

Note the word *trust*. While similar in many ways, a trust is different from a will. If you have a trust in place for your business and its assets, no one can claim your business interests after you die. That's because a trust legally holds ownership of your business and specifies who will inherit it in the event of your death.

Drawing one up generally does not cost a lot, and will save your beneficiary and business a lot of time and money down the line.

Imagine Mike O'Keefe and I operate Expert Business Advice for 50 years. One day, I eat the most delicious pizza ever made and die of pleasure. If I don't have any immediate family members alive then, and if I don't have a trust, my share of the business won't go to Mike. It will go to my nearest living relative, or worse, the government! Eeek! I would come back as a zombie to prevent that from happening!

Beyond the benefit of a seamless transition of your business or stake in a business to whomever you choose, a trust will also provide tax breaks for the person you leave it to. That is, it may avoid inheritance taxes. It will keep the transition simple, limit the publicity surrounding your death, and ensure that your family members, employees, or business partners don't end up in a court fight.

If you decide to develop a business trust, here are some tips that will help you avoid some common pitfalls:

- Be 100 percent correct about any names you mention in your document. If the names on the business, assets (e.g. real estate), and the names of beneficiaries in the trust don't match perfectly, you're creating problems which will cost you or your beneficiaries time and money to rectify in the future, if they can rectify them at all.

- Keep all your business agreements up-to-date, always. Business licenses and other contracts can expire. Make a calendar of renewal and expiration dates, at least for your most important agreements.

- Ensure you keep your business's organizational house in order so you can rest in peace.

Keyman and buy/sell provisions

There are a couple other things you should consider doing in this context. Say you and your spouse own a company that makes a face soap that has little black abrasive flakes in it—the Pepper-Dermis Soap Company. The two of you run the business so efficiently that the loss of either one of you would be catastrophic.

Alas, one day, while out collecting gravel for your Pepper-Dermis soap, your spouse gets run over by a rhino that escaped from the local zoo. Not only are you emotionally devastated, but there's no way that you can run the business by yourself or train someone else to fill your spouse's role. Thankfully, you had the foresight to buy what's quaintly called Keyman Insurance (the name is slowly evolving toward Key Person Insurance nowadays). It pays out agreed sums to help your business survive the death of a key person in the business. If you have individuals in your business who have a unique skill set, or are responsible for the majority of the business's profits, consider buying Keyman insurance.

Finally, it's wise to have a buy/sell agreement, also commonly known as a buyout agreement, if you are a co-owner in a business. It's a legally binding contract among co-owners that defines what happens if one of the owners dies or has to leave the business for any reason. The most basic buyout agreements articulate who can buy a departing partner's share of the business (and in what order the share will be offered), what events will trigger the buyout (death, desire, personal bankruptcy, etc.), and what price will be paid for the departing partner's share.

This is not "nice to have" stuff: It's necessary. As owners of Expert Business Advice, we have living trusts, Keyman insurance, and a buyout agreement in place. You need to consider doing likewise if you own, or plan to own, a business. Most entrepreneurs don't have time to worry about the end of their life because they're too busy planning the rest of theirs. However, if you spend so much time building a business today, don't you want to protect your legacy and have a say in the way you want it to continue, when you're gone?

S.G.

Check, Please! How to Wind Down a Business

How to close or dissolve a business efficiently and legally.

JUST BECAUSE YOU'RE CLOSING YOUR DOORS, it doesn't necessarily have to be because your business is tanking. Sometimes, businesses owners just decide they don't want to do business any more. Maybe their business is small and they can't or don't want to find a buyer to carry on. Or it's time to retire, or they want to focus on another new company start-up. Or the company's outlook is gloomy due to industry shifts or other factors. A key distinction is whether you are closing in the red (owe people money that you cannot pay) or whether you close in the black (when upon completion, there will be no outstanding debt or liability related to the business).

In any case, if you get to the point where you want to wind down your company, there are a few things you must do beside turning off the lights, locking the doors, and walking away. Some of these steps are obvious, but others are not. It's imperative now to work with your attorney (and probably also your accountant and tax advisor, plus others) to close your business the right way, so you stay on the good side of the law and avoid penalties down the road. Needless to say, you must observe the procedures and laws that apply at your company's official site of business, so take the points below as general guides that may vary based on where you are headquartered.

Close the business officially. The specific actions you must take to do this vary according to the type of business structure you picked when you started up, and also the wind-down clauses in your founding documents. If you are a sole proprietor, all you have to do is stand up tall, click your ruby slippers' heels together three times and say out loud, *"There's NO place like MY business."* At that moment, there will literally be no place like your business, because it will have been dissolved. (Okay, you don't have to do that.) Your sole proprietorship closes when you say it does; you just have to file the proper paperwork. If, however, there are multiple owners, as in partnerships, limited liability companies (LLCs) and corporations, you must follow the dissolution process outlined in your founding documents. Regardless of the process, document the dissolution on paper.

Dissolve the business with the government. It's important that you file paperwork to close your business with the government, to keep yourself from continuing to owe business taxes and filing fees. Typically, you can use the same place or website you used to incorporate for this.

Cancel licenses and permits. You must also cancel all the licenses, permits, and trade names you won't be using in the future. If someone else starts doing business in your name, you could be on the hook for paying the taxes and penalties. Canceling is the same as filing; you just go where you filed and complete the cancelation. The process is simple and easy.

Take care of any obligations to employees. Find out what you must do early on. Your local laws will specify when you must notify employees about the business closing as well as when final pay checks, unused leave compensation and so forth are due.

Pay your taxes and debts. When paying final taxes and debts, always pay your taxes first. If it's looking like you're going to have trouble paying your taxes and debts, ask your attorney to try to negotiate your figure down. If she succeeds, it's likely that you'll end up owing less overall, even after paying her fee.

Notify your employees, landlord, lessors, customers and creditors. If you've been in business a while and your decision to close wasn't an easy one to make, this can be the most painful part of closing. It's best to be honest, but not hasty. If you still have contractual obligations for deliveries of products or services, and you think your employees might all just walk out and never come back when you tell them you're closing, ensure that you can fulfill your contractual obligations before you notify them. If you anticipate emotional reactions, gently remind your employees that libel or slander is a serious crime, something they don't want to have to deal with while they find a new job. If you really think you might have an issue, it might even be worth hiring an off-duty law enforcement officer to hang out in your lobby for the last few weeks. Typically, this can be coordinated through your local law enforcement agency.

If your business has any leases, ensure you follow whatever terms are in your lease agreements. If you have corporate credit cards and accounts, cancel or close those. It might be best to leave certain cards or accounts open a little longer, in case you have last-minute closing expenses.

Customers should be notified as soon as possible, but not before your employees, to avoid leaks, rumors and so forth. Fulfill any obligations you owe your customers, or offer them full or partial refunds on products or services you cannot provide due to closure.

Line up secure storage for key documents. Find out how long you must store relevant tax, corporate and other documents and make appropriate arrangements for that period of time. Shred and dispose of anything not worth keeping.

It's always best to try to handle your closure with as much grace and dignity as you can, treating everyone affected by it with professional respect. The last thing you want is a smeared reputation or ongoing personal liability, simply because you botched your closing.

S.G.

CHAPTER V

Common Mistakes

Don't Be That Guy or Gal: Ten Common Mistakes

*Sometimes, even the most ethical entrepreneurs
can get into legal trouble.*

STARTING AND GROWING A BUSINESS draws on practically all your resources. If your background hasn't exposed you to entrepreneurial thinking, you'll have lots to learn. One piece of advice comes out again and again when you ask entrepreneurs for some of their favorite tips: *Know what you don't know.* And as you'll see below, if you are short on that wisdom, you may make serious mistakes with the best of intentions. So here are ten common mistakes you can avoid just by knowing about them!

Not being self-disciplined. Self-discipline is essential. Don't think running your own business means going home early whenever you want. Or not sticking to budgets and spending limits, paying random bonuses with extra money rather than saving it. Or treating employees inconsistently. Or blurring the lines of employer/employee roles.

Not using contracts, or not reading them if they are used. Likewise, inconsistent record keeping, especially in accounting. If you cook your own books to make the business look profitable, you are only cheating yourself.

Not consulting with a lawyer for key issues or important business document review. Don't make this mistake, because the consequences are potentially huge. All businesses start the same way: as ideas and paperwork. If you're going to invest your life, time and money in a business, don't you think it's worth starting it out the right way and ensuring that paperwork experts get a chance to look at it? It won't cost that much, because they are efficient. After all, they study business paperwork for a living. Their highly trained eyes and years of thinking about the best interests of their clients will always catch something that would take you hours or days to catch, if you catch it at all. Putting it a different way, if you hesitate because of costs, consider the price of undoing your do-it-yourself lawyering if you get things wrong.

Not incorporating, or choosing the wrong corporate structure. You attorney can guide you based on your vision and plans. The easiest way to start a small business is with a sole proprietorship. The taxes are easily manageable and there is very little paperwork. Unfortunately, if someone accidentally injures herself using your product, she could end up owning your house, all your stuff, and all your money via a lawsuit. Incorporation means protection for the business owner(s). Protect yourself and your immediate family by incorporating. If you know you will never eventually take your company public, a limited liability company (LLC) is likely your best bet, due to the ease of incorporation and lower taxes than with full incorporation (LLCs cannot go public). Not limiting your liability by forming an LLC or corporation is asking for trouble.

Failing to patent, trademark, or copyright material. Earlier we discussed the hand-made jewelry designer who found out the hard way that she wasn't the only one with a creative eye and a great idea. This can happen with slogans, songs, images, logos, icons, products, procedures, or a million other things related to building a business and brand. Don't try to do the research yourself; I guarantee that you won't know all the places to look. There are corporate attorneys who specialize in patenting, trademarking and copyrighting. In fact, in many cases, that's all they do. Think of it like this: Do you really want to build an entire business around something, only to find out the hard way that you're not the first to do it, and the person who was first *did* protect themselves and their idea with a patent, trademark or copyright? That, my friends, is a bad day to be a business owner.

Not having a formal agreement between owners. Owner agreements don't have to be long. In fact, I think ours is only a couple pages. Mike O'Keefe was my college roommate and the best man at my wedding, but despite our history, when we started Expert Business Advice, LLC together, even we had a formal operating and ownership agreement. It basically just puts in writing who the owners are, how much we each own, what our responsibilities are, what happens if one of us dies or elects to leave the company, how major business decisions will be handled, etc. Also, we are not 50/50 (equal) owners. This can sometimes cause issues for a group of friends who all want to own equal shares, but you must find some way to make it unequal, or you'll suffer death by stalemate. If two people own a business together and want to be as equal as possible, I recommend a 51/49 percent ownership split. The money is practically equal, but when decisions must be made, they can always be enacted. If you cannot decide who will be the majority owner, use the oldest tipping mechanism in the book—flip a coin!

Starting a business with a large loan, but not understanding the terms of the loan or how to manage it. Just because you get a hefty business loan doesn't mean you can start throwing money around. As we have seen, you really need to read the fine print to ensure you don't have to start paying that loan back right away. And if you do get a huge loan, don't start hiring all your friends to work at your business. It takes careful analysis to determine how many employees a business requires to run optimally. You friends may think you are wicked awesome for hiring them, but the test of your friendship might come when your loan is spent. I hope for your sake at least one of them has a comfortable sofa.

Working on your new business idea at your old job. Say you design and build widgets. You've worked at your job for ten years and just love it. Now you've developed a completely revolutionary widget design on your own, in spare moments at work. It will transform the widget industry. You don't have a non-compete agreement with your employer, so you decide to start your own widget business based on your new design. On your last day at your old job, you print out the designs for your new widget and take the schematics home.

Unfortunately, some time later, you get a letter from your old company's attorney, claiming that they own your new widget design! I hate to be the bearer of bad news, but I'm afraid most courts would find that your old company does own your new widget. Here's why: You created your new widget on their time, using their equipment, while they were paying you to design and build widgets for them. You even printed off the schematics on their printer. Oh yeah, they own your widget.

If this scenario rings any bells in your head, meet with an experienced business lawyer and check out your situation. It would be better to figure out how to develop prototypes of your new company's product under conditions that guarantee the new products are yours, than to have them swept up in costly lawsuits and heartbreak.

Thinking you know enough. Lack of continuing education or continuing improvement can trip you up at any time. Just because you made it through the first year does not mean you kick back and rest on your accomplishments.

Not keeping records and documents in perfect order. Do yourself a favor and make your paperwork a model of organized efficiency.

There you have it. Steer clear of these mistakes and you'll up your odds of success!

S.G. and M.R.M.

Isn't a Tort Made of Chocolate?

*Torts are wrongdoings made by or against individuals
or businesses. Be alert for them.*

YOU'VE PROBABLY HEARD THE WORD *TORT* at some point or another. Simply put, a tort is wrongdoing committed by or against people or businesses. Common types of torts involving businesses include fraud, embezzlement, unfair competition, misrepresentation, breach of fiduciary duty (in a corporation, when a director acts against shareholders' interests), embezzlement, equity-stripping or minority owner squeeze-outs, product liability, malpractice, negligence, etc. These are the things that high-drama novels and movies are made of!

Torts can occur when a business is solely responsible for wrong (e.g., product liability), but can also involve responsibility for a wrong by the business, its owners, its employees and other individuals involved with it, in any combination. (e.g., negligence or misrepresentation). Torts can also include wrongs against the business, its owners, its employees or other individuals involved with it (e.g., civil theft or fraud).

What to do if accused

Valid or not, accusations of torts can be catastrophic to your business. Businesses can be accused of interfering with the operation of another business; or of acting in an oppressive, harmful, unscrupulous or oppressive manner to their customers; or a host of other things.

If your business is accused of some kind of wrongdoing, do not respond directly. Bring your business attorney in on the situation. Typically, if you are getting sued by someone or another business, it's too late to stop legal action. If it turns out your business is in the wrong, either accidentally or deliberately, your business attorney can often negotiate with the plaintiff and secure a more favorable verdict, a dismissal or a settlement that is less damaging to your business's operations and reputation.

Let's look at two common types of torts committed by and against businesses, so as a new or prospective business owner, you can keep yourself protected.

Misrepresentation

Remember when you wrote that business plan in hopes of taking it to a bank to secure your start-up or expansion loan? Hopefully all your numbers were true and accurate. If you padded or inflated them, you may have been committing a very serious, and regrettably common business tort: misrepresentation. Depending on the circumstances and the results of the misrepresentation, it could carry serious consequences. Many entities are very good at detecting misrepresentations and aggressively pursuing their rights. The wronged parties will not think twice about going after an individual or entity that has misrepresented material facts, which could lead to additional risks.

There are three types of misrepresentation, in ascending order of liability risk:

- **Innocent** Just what it sounds like: It's an honest, good faith and unintentional mistake made without the intention to harm. This has a very low liability risk.

- **Negligent** An unintentional mistake made due to the failure to follow established or reasonable standards of care. So while you are not intentionally misrepresenting a fact, you are not making a good-faith attempt to provide the truth. This carries significant liability risk.

- **Fraudulent** An intentional misrepresentation of a material fact. Needless to say, this act risks extreme liability.

Small businesses are most often the victims of these types of torts. To help you recognize the most serious version, fraudulent misrepresentation, take a look at the actions that define it:

- A false statement (or concealment) was made.

- It was a statement of a "material fact", i.e., its content would be important in decision making, vs. trivial content.

- The person making the statement knew it to be false or had reckless disregard about its truth.

- The misrepresentation was made with the intention of getting the other party to act.

- The other party did rely on the statement.

- Due to this reliance on the false statement, the other party suffered damages.

Examples are the classic bait-and-switch maneuver you might encounter when selling a business or buying goods or services. You as the business owner are shown and told one thing, but then the product or service that is actually delivered is vastly different. In that case you could be the victim of a tort.

Tortious or intentional interference with contractual relations

Most business between people and entities will not (and should not) occur without a contract. Remember, contracts are not only the lengthy agreements with signatures and amendments we picture. Invoices, purchase orders, employment agreements, owner agreements, and letters of intent can be contracts too. Even a check exchanged can be considered as a constructive contract in the right circumstances. It is a document that you sign and deliver that indicates that you agree to pay another party the amount written in, for the purpose annotated on it, that can be accepted by the other party. Hence the rationale for serious penalties behind forgery, mail or check fraud.

In the realm of torts affecting contractual relations, even petty behavior can lead to big trouble. Suppose a competitor spreads an untrue rumor about a you or your business to one of his suppliers, and the supplier decides not to renew her contract with you. That's a tort. When you find out, your competitor, called a "tortfeasor", could be facing multiple suits.

To be liable for tortious or intentional interference with contractual relations, generally the following requirements apply:

- A valid contract or contractual relationships existed between the two parties.

- The third party (the tortfeasor, i.e., liable party, violator and generally bad person) had knowledge of the contract or contractual relationship.

- The third party intended to convince or induce one of the parties to the contract to commit a breach.

- The third party was not privileged or authorized in any way to induce the breach.

- The contract was in fact breached.

- The non-breaching party suffered some sort of measurable damages.

Negligence

Negligence is basically the failure to do what you reasonably should have done. It is one of the most common types of torts, either by itself or as an element of other torts (as for example in negligent misrepresentation). It is very important to note that negligence arises out of *careless* behavior, and not intentional actions.

Generally, to be liable for negligence, the following requirements apply (and incidentally, this case is a version of a law school example):

- **Duty** The liable party had a reasonable duty to the other party (a shopkeeper has a duty not to place hidden, cobra-filled snake pits in her shop).

- **Breach** The liable party breached that duty (the shopkeeper does in fact place a hidden snake pit in the shop, complete with cobras).

- **Causation** The breach by the liable party either actually or legally causes harm to the other party (a shopper enters the shop, falls in snake pit, is bitten by a snake and dies).

- **Damages** As a result of this harm, the other party has incurred monetary damages that require compensation (the shopper, now dead, is no longer able to earn income and provide for her family, so the shopper's family therefore requires monetary compensation).

There are many specific types of negligence and negligence-related torts in each jurisdiction (including criminal negligence, gross negligence, comparative negligence, contributory negligence, vicarious liability or negligence per se). Some of the most common types of negligence torts in relation to businesses are property liability (slips and falls or injuries in a business); product liability (defective products); accidents (vehicle or industrial accidents); or malpractice (errors, omissions or medical malpractice). As an entrepreneur, you need to review and follow the reasonable standards of care expected in your industry and take steps to mitigate risk (via insurance, safety standards and equipment, signage, etc.). It would be wise to ask your attorney to help you identify risk exposures and address your need for prevention and protection accordingly.

Owning and running a business means that you will be executing transactions depending on the honesty, fair dealing and responsible behavior of many individuals and entities. Sometimes bad things happen, sometimes people act badly, sometimes you will not be able to resolve the situation and sometimes you may be forced into the legal system. If you use common sense, make ethical and morally sound decisions and understand the standards you are held too, you will steer clear of liability for torts. As we've said, if you suspect or you are the victim of a wrong by another party, a tort has most likely occurred. Take it very seriously and contact your attorney.

Finally, torts are not cheese or wine. They do not get better with age, regardless of which side you are on. As I advise my clients, "Go ugly early." Get out in front of any incident: Address it as soon as possible and be pro-active. It will really help you and your business in any damage control if the victim feels like this event is a priority to you. You will also establish your business reputation as one not to be messed with by those seeking to take advantage.

S.G. and M.R.M.

Product Liability

*An important piece of your corporate
protection puzzle.*

WE ALL LIKE TO THINK that when we buy something, it will do what it's supposed to do without causing harm. Yet we've all had experiences or heard of cases in which bad things happened: the super-duper gadget with a jagged handle which cut your hand, the faulty design of a tool that caused accidents and injuries, the cosmetic that burned your skin because the instructions didn't say to wash it off after one minute.

If your company is a manufacturer, distributor, supplier, retailer or other entity involved in the process of making products available to the public, you may be obliged to compensate for injury caused by defective merchandise you have been involved with. Generally, only tangible products are the focus here—things you can touch. We cannot give you hard and fast advice here, because product liability standards vary by product, industry and jurisdiction. In this aspect of business, you really must consult an attorney with expertise in the topic.

The sorts of complaints that are brought in a product liability suit include negligence, breach of warranty and what is called strict liability. Let's take a quick look at them.

- **Negligence** Exactly what it sounds like. There was a duty owed, then a breach of that duty. The breach caused an injury and there are quantifiable damages suffered from the injury. For example, a taxi driver fails to obey traffic laws, the taxi is at fault in an accident, and passengers are injured as a result.

- **Breach of warranty** The seller specifically states that a product can do something, but the product is unable to fulfill that representation. For example, a consumer purchases a product labeled as a DVD player, but the product will not play DVDs. This can also fall under mis-representation.

- **Strict Liability** This sets a much higher standard for the regular man-ufacturers and sellers, and it provides significantly more protection for the consumers. The injured party must only prove that the product was defective and dangerous when sold, and that the defect caused the injury. There is no requirement to prove fault or negligence against the seller. This may seem like lawyers have pushed the law too far, but the rules are designed to protect individuals from large companies. The law makes it easier for ordinary consumers to prove liability against large businesses, something that otherwise might be impossible, given the businesses' massive and well-funded legal teams.

Here's a *who-what-when-where-how-why* rundown of basics.

Who?

All businesses that produce, handle or affect a product before it reaches the final consumer can be liable. Yes, that means you, even if you are only reselling items on eBay (though you'd have to be selling things regularly to bear liability; single, or infrequent sales are not affected). While many businesses, especially service-based businesses, may not have tangible products, they may still be liable under similar service-related laws. As we'll see in the next section, other variations of this liability apply to them: malpractice for a doctor or lawyer, errors or omissions for financial or real estate professionals, premises liability for hotels or social event locations.

What?

You and/or the business can be liable and/or responsible (i.e., made to pay or even face criminal charges in extreme cases) if someone is injured (i.e., dam-aged, harmed either physically, mentally, or financially) because of your product. The ways products are found to be defective are:

- **A manufacturing defect** Perhaps you put the product together wrongly or put some bad parts in. Examples are most recalls, where only certain cars, phones or other products are recalled due to faulty sub-components, such as a particular model of car sold with a particu-lar brand of tires that had a tendency to explode and cause the vehicle to roll over.

- **A design defect** There could be a design defect (you designed a prod-uct that does really bad things). For example, your car design put the gas tank in the rear, but if the car is rear-ended, it explodes. Or the product's formulation has unintended side effects: This pill will make some of your pain go away, but it will also likely stop your heart (so take two and call us in the morning?).

- **Or failure to warn** Perhaps you forgot to mention that your product did SOMETHING ELSE too. Examples: we forgot to advise that tobacco products also cause cancer, or we forgot to mention that coffee was extremely hot.

When

Liability can arise at any time throughout the *normal* operation or use of your product. For example, a car manufacturer would be liable if its car burst into flames during routine driving, but not if it burst into flames when a driver was trying to jump it across the Grand Canyon. There are specific limits of *when*, defined by product, industry and jurisdiction. These limits will also define time in the form of a statute of limitations. They say that after a certain time, you are no longer liable for damages related to this product.

Where

Liability is confined to use within the course of normal operation. If you burn out your dog's hair clipper motor while trying to trim the hedge, don't bother filing for damages. These things are usually defined on a case-by-case basis.

How

Liability cases are brought as demands against a business, claims to insurance policies or lawsuits. Remember, a case can be brought against anyone in the supply chain. As a general rule, when filing a claim (from the injured person's side), the strategy is to go after everyone and then focus on the easy targets and the deep pockets (i.e., parties with the ability to pay). From the perspective of the injured person, the goal is compensation for injury (medical bills, loss of income, pain and suffering, etc.). The person does not care much where the compensation comes from. So be prepared: As a business owner it is not a question of IF you will face a claim, but WHEN you will have to.

Why

Why do product liability laws exist? The answer's simple: consumer protection. Yes, this area of law has spawned ambulance-chasing lawyers and others who can give the profession an extremely bad rap, based on outrageous cases (e.g., a fortune awarded for not telling that consumer the coffee was hot). And it's too bad that almost every quality-driven business will face a claim at some point. But the public policy behind the way the law is written is to create financial incentives for businesses to do the right thing and to produce safe products. As a whole the system works: It is because of this system that tobacco products now carry warning labels and are not marketed to children, our buildings are no longer built with "fire resistant" asbestos and our homes are no longer painted with the cheaper lead-based paint, all of which were proven to be extremely harmful to the consumers.

At this point, I imagine you are ready to return to the Insurance section of this book, and perhaps the phonebook, to make sure your product liability coverage is adequate. And that, plus your continued vigilance over your company's delivery of safe experiences with your products, is your best strategy.

M.R.M.

Other Forms of Liability

*Mistakes can and do happen. It's better
to be pro-active than sorry.*

NOT ALL LIABILITY IS PRODUCT LIABILITY. There are a number of other forms of responsibility and liability you should be aware of. These types of liability relate to intangible products (things you cannot physically touch), and to services.

Malpractice or Professional Liability Generally, this affects regulated professionals who fail to meet their profession's standards of practice. Most professionals are required to carry the related insurance. Examples are doctors, lawyers and accountants.

Errors and Omissions This is very similar to malpractice liability, primarily related to transactional businesses in industries with more paperwork than products. You may or may not be required to carry this type of insurance. Examples include financial services, real estate brokers and bookkeepers.

Premises and Property This applies to any brick and mortar business and covers the slips and falls in the store, the freak accidents, etc. If you are in this field, you absolutely must insure against this risk. In certain jurisdictions, it is the single largest risk to businesses. Accidents happen, and, yes, there are con men and scam artists out there that prey on small businesses by staging accidents.

Further, this liability has been extended in some jurisdictions to include areas immediately surrounding your business, such as a parking lot. For example, if you know that more than one person has been assaulted in your parking lot and you fail to warn customers, properly light the area after dark or even possibly fail to hire appropriate security, your business could be found to be liable, if another customer were to be assaulted.

Data and Confidential Information This risk affects any business that keeps or has access to confidential information. It could be specifically protected business information related to the operations or practices of one of your suppliers, or it could be clients' sensitive information like credit card account numbers. As you know, this is a fast-growing risk area for businesses, with criminals targeting some of the largest and most well-funded businesses all over the world. Consider insuring against data theft and planning for recovery from it when designing your operations.

Workers' Compensation Any business with employees has to address this. Each jurisdiction has unique laws or rules related to your duties and responsibilities. Basically, you have to keep your employees safe at work and compensate them if they are injured in the course of normal business operations.

Vehicles If your employees drive motor vehicles as part of their job duties, this affects you. Each jurisdiction will have specific laws and rules related to vehicle accident liability. This is an area that is very often overlooked until it is too late.

The most common example is small brick-and-mortar retail or service business, say an ice cream shop or doctor's office. They run out of spoons or printer paper, so the business sends an employee to the store. On the way to the store the employee has an accident and is at fault. The business now shares liability/responsibility (i.e., can be sued and made to pay) for the accident, because the employee was driving within the course of his employment. This common example is an especially big deal in that most businesses would not have any insurance to cover this situation, thinking their employees do not drive as part of their regular job. So why should you pay the high cost of the additional insurance to cover vehicle accidents by employees? The damage payments could be a game changer for a small business. Note: This is also why so many small businesses (including mine) pay a premium for the delivery of supplies directly to the office.

Time to take a deep breath. Yes, you face a lot of liability out there as a business owner. Remember, these sections were written by an attorney who deals with these situations every day. So go back and reread the section on business insurance, then make an appointment to sit down with your insurance agent. (Note: Insure your risks, and make sure they are covered. But be aware that the insurance agent works for the insurance company. And the insurance company is in business to make a profit…).

M.R.M.

CHAPTER VI

International Law

Starting to Think about International Business

Expanding your business in international markets can be very exciting. Ensure you know the right way to do it.

WHEN YOU BUY GOODS these days, there's a good chance many of the items on offer originated outside your country. Traveling abroad, you cannot avoid seeing global brands on everything. Reading or watching the news, you are struck by the ingenious ways one-person companies have found to open businesses halfway around the world to help improve people's lives there. Advances in technology, communications and logistics have opened the global marketplace, and it seems almost everybody is in it or thinking about entering it, whether selling or buying.

It's an exciting time to be in global business, but it can have its challenges. One of them is that each country or trade zone is governed by its own sets of regulations for conducting business, particularly when importing or exporting products. If you want to do business in another country, you must abide by its rules. Add in the mix of language, culture and geographical influences we all encounter abroad, and it's a heady cocktail to savor.

Mike O'Keefe and I started a U.S. company a few years back that specialized in outsourcing small motors and related components, as well as large-volume lighting for hotel chains. China was known then for cheap labor in manufacturing, so we started and built our business there. We soon found out that only Chinese citizens can own businesses in China. It is a way for the Chinese government to ensure that the gross domestic product (money made in China) stays in China, in the form of Chinese taxes. We were only allowed to do business with Chinese factories and sourcing specialists in order to make our business work.

Starting out with solid facts and plans

When you start thinking about doing business outside your headquarter country, it's best to remember a few key tips.

- Doing business abroad will be unlike doing business at home. Don't take anything for granted.

- Read up about the target country in general, so you have a feel for current events, politics, trends and the economy, geography, history and culture, including its customs and courtesies.

- Educate yourself about your own industry sector in the target country via trade journals, online resources, your government's commercial attachés.

- Get reliable tax advice. For instance, if you are a U.S. company, no matter where in the world you operate, you must still follow U.S. regulations regarding compliance, financial and legal obligations. You must still pay U.S. taxes, even for revenue from your offices outside the U.S., as long as you are a company incorporated within the U.S.

- With all your research complete, draw up a complete business plan and review it with a tax expert and a lawyer familiar with the target country. If your usual attorney is not versed in the area, he can recommend a qualified one.

Scoping out the target country

If you plan to send one of your employees or an official representative abroad to scout and develop business contacts, ensure you've done your homework on that person too.

- Will she project a professional, positive image of your company?

- Is she a flexible, resourceful, comfortable traveler?

- Does she speak languages that will be useful?

- Does she have proper travel documents, and have you checked visa requirements?

- Is she competent in her job function so she can develop contacts, interview prospects, collect information, get pricing, give specifications, etc. properly?

- Will she will behave ethically and responsibly while on the assignment? If you are a U.S. company and she commits a crime or violates any business ethics laws while overseas and you didn't conduct your own background check on her, the U.S. Department of Justice and the Securities and Exchange Commission (never mind the target country) could hold you and your business responsible for her violation.

Going global can be very exciting, but also very confusing, challenging and downright risky. The cost of consulting with an international business attorney and tax advisor will save countless headaches and is merely a fraction of what you could pay if you get into trouble. Stay on the safe side and let experts keep you prepared and advised.

S.G.

Working Though Your International Business Plan

With this plan in hand you'll have a firm foundation for business abroad.

MANY OF THE STARTUPS or young businesses we meet with tell me they consider international business as something reserved for jet-set executives and Fortune 500 companies. However, they may be doing international business without really knowing it.

Some of the most common, yet not highly visible, examples are entrepreneurs who order products directly from international suppliers, even if it is just one component of the item they eventually sell. If it is supplied from across an international border, then you are doing international business. Or perhaps you have a retail business that offers online or catalog sales. Your consumers could be anywhere in the world, buying via the world wide web, an environment that crosses traditional international borders with a click.

Of course, there's also the more visible global business world: the physical transportation of products, establishment of branches, set-ups with distribution partners or sales reps, ex-patriot assignments, financial transactions or even the execution of documents. No wonder there are scads of regulations in play.

Despite the fact that the *international* aspect of this business sounds—and is—really cool, it significantly increases the complexity and risks you face. If you see opportunity out there, you will encounter many of the other concerns discussed throughout this book, with the added layer of at least one completely different country (with perhaps significantly different jurisdiction) to also consider.

So it should come as no surprise that we emphatically recommend that you educate yourself, get reliable advice, and develop a business plan before you make any commitment to international business. By that we mean a plan for your first venture, and then separate plans for new territories as you expand.

Major considerations to address in your international business plan

Not all, but many of the factors you'll need to think through are legal matters. Some are financial, and then there's a whole rainbow of other things. Since in many ways these things are inseparable, we want to get you thinking in a broad, long-term mindset. Here are some of the major items to consider about potential international business.

Legal Systems If you must use your target country's legal system, can you even do so? Will it work? Is it cost effective and reasonably transparent? Are you able to reasonably predict the outcome? Do you have qualified legal representation there? Things will be simpler in a country with a legal system similar to yours and with established professionals (lawyers or barristers) who speak your language. In contrast, doing business in a distant country, one that speaks another language and is based on tribal systems where you are expected to pay an unknown tribute amount to the local establishment for an unknown result, will demand more patience, flexibility, caution, and long-term commitment.

Political Systems What is the target country's system of government at all levels—national, regional and local? How would they affect your business? How stable are those political systems? What roles do corruption, bribery and organized crime play? If systems are likely to change, what is the probable effect on your business? Stable systems tend to support more business, with less risk and generally lower average returns on investment (due to higher competition), as compared to many developing or recently peaceful countries that have significantly lower stability, higher risk, but also higher potential returns. There may be good news for entrepreneurs considering the latter countries: any of the international investment treaties discussed below will have significant incentives for businesses to encourage them to invest there.

Labor Standards Many companies, small and large, have outsourced various parts of their businesses overseas: manufacturing operations to China, technical support to India or documentary support to South America. The reason? Reduced labor costs and benefits like 24/7 workdays. Consider questions like these. What are the local employment requirements? What are the wage rates and what's forecasted for them? Are these cost effective for your operations? What is the quality of the workforce population? Is there any potential for becoming involved in undesirable practices like child labor, or situations where you may attract bad business publicity for operating out of these specific countries?

Local Culture and Other Considerations Will the local culture support or threaten your business model? For example, in some cultures, copying is the highest form of praise. What impact will that have on your activity? Are there language barriers or educational barriers that would affect business? What is the local work schedule? Are there any religious, tribal or other factors that need to be considered? The examples in this category are rich and abundant, from differences in workdays, daily working hours, translated product names that have offensive meanings in local slang; plus vast cultural differences in management, hierarchy and communication methods.

Environmental Issues What are the local concerns and regulations related to the environment? If your home country's rules are tougher, then which should you follow? What is the potential for damage from a natural disaster (earthquake, monsoon) or an environmental emergency? Are there ethical dilemmas related to locally legal but admittedly harmful practices? Waste generation and disposal, sustainable development, emissions, long-term damage and potential liability related to harm done are very real issues here. Examples of these tough issues are in every day's news.

Infrastructure This is an area where it pays to see things first-hand if your target country is underdeveloped or starting its ascent. Are roads, utilities, communication systems and port or rail facilities reliable? Do other companies with experience in your target country have tales to tell about patchwork solutions, and are you willing to work that way? What future improvements are planned, and who's funding them?

Import/Export Trade Regulations Some very complex considerations get involved here, and you need to evaluate them extremely carefully. Key factors include your product, country, shipping method, prices, etc. These could be affected by tariffs, quotas, trade agreements, standards regulation, regional preferences, popular opinion, etc. Your product may not sell well vs. locally made products, or import fees or taxes may make it too expensive to compete well, or it may not meet technical standards of quality or measurement. On the other hand, you could benefit from programs that give incentives to invest in the target country's workforce training and development, or from other sorts of consideration.

Transactions Costs and Exchange Rates Transaction costs include the freight and the extra layers needed to supervise transport of supplies and products; the risk involved in potential loss, damage or delay of shipments; variation in currency exchange rates that could affect profitability; costs to meet local regulatory and accounting requirements; local tax considerations and more.

Major Tax Considerations International tax strategy and planning is a huge, complicated deal, with many Fortune 500 companies reaping significant profits as a result. Many countries, including Ireland, Bermuda, the Cayman Islands, Hong Kong and Luxembourg, among others, structure their tax codes to attract international business and investment. As your revenues increase along with your international presence, this can become a long-term strategic consideration.

At this point you probably are having second thoughts, at least about pulling together a sound business plan. Don't feel pressed to rush through this, and do get advice from your network and your legal and tax advisors to help fill in the blanks. Doing this will reduce the number of blanks left, highlighting the remaining ones, so you can see what you'll need to find out and weigh before you take binding decisions.

M.R.M. and S.G.

Nationalization of Businesses

*You may think your business is far too small to
attract a government's attention in this regard.
But if your activity is deemed strategic
to a host government, think twice
and plan ahead.*

NATIONALIZATION IS A CATASTROPHIC BUSINESS EVENT. It happens when a governmental agency takes possession, control and ownership of a private business interest, and may or may not include compensation for the private business. Nationalization is not just the headline-stealing take-over of an oil field by a rogue dictator; it can happen to you. You see it in developing nations as part of regime or political changes, but also quite commonly in industrialized countries. It is also known as reverse privatization.

Eminent Domain/Resumption/Expropriation This happens when private property is taken for public use. The most common form of "nationalization" is eminent domain, used for infrastructure projects like roads or high-tension wires. It is also used when changes in zoning laws require new uses for a particular property. This is an area in which you can be affected drastically, even if you are not operating internationally. New zoning ordinances can restrict the size and type of signage you use, impose obligations to make your business wheelchair accessible, or put you out of business, if for example you own a pub and the property is re-zoned to be alcohol free.

Emergency Industry Nationalization In times of war or catastrophe a government can take control of specific industries, such as airport security following the September 11 attacks in the U.S. or the railroads during World War II in a number of countries.

Corporate Control or Bailout In troubled economic times, governments may step in and prevent a company from failing by taking control of the company or making direct investments into it. This is done because the company is viewed as too critical to fail, due to the product produced or to long-term economic effects. Examples include the British nationalization of Rolls Royce in 1971, or the U.S. bailout of the airline industry.

The laws covering nationalization in industrialized countries are local to the jurisdiction. In developing nations, they could be subject to existing laws or created through political change. Nationalization, the possibility of compensation if it happens, and your rights as a business or property owner are potential major risks you must take into consideration in your business planning, wherever you are located.

M.R.M.

Treaties 101

*You don't need to be a diplomat
to be involved with them.*

WHAT IS A TREATY, ANYWAY? Think of it as a contract between two or more countries or international organizations. You may find related words like *protocols*, *conventions*, and *pacts* used instead. Treaties document agreements among the parties to do, or not to do, or to obligate themselves to either very specific points or very general guidelines.

The system of international laws that regulates cross-border business is collectively called International Commercial Law. If you plan on buying or selling goods internationally, you should know about the United Nations Convention on Contracts for the International Sale of Goods (CISG; sometimes called the Vienna Convention) and the World Trade Organization (WTO).

United Nations Convention on Contracts for the International Sale of Goods (CISG)

The CISG is the convention for the sale of goods that cross international borders. If you own a U.S. business which makes birdhouses, and you buy all of your materials from Amazon.com, eBay.com or other reputable importers, you don't need to worry about this. Those merchants have already dealt with all applicable regulations for the materials they resell to you.

There is one thing to keep in mind with the CISG: not all countries abide by it. Because it's a United Nations organization, only members of the United Nations honor it. If you decide to directly import from or export to another country, make sure you research that country's regulations adequately. Generally, most countries in Africa, Asia, Europe (Eastern and Western), Latin America, and the Caribbean participate in CISG. The United Nations hosts a website fully dedicated to CISG, also known as UNCITRAL (visit uncitral.org). They provide basic facts about international trade, along with frequently asked questions. The site is currently published in six languages.

The World Trade Organization (WTO) is organized under a treaty, but it functions as more of a centralized record keeper or secretary. It supports international trade and provides a common structure for trade relations between contracting parties. The main objective of the WTO is to consider issues like tariff classifications, product nature, intended use, commercial value, price, and sustainability in order to minimize discrimination between imported and domestic products. The WTO has no actual authority to create or enforce trade agreements. All treaties are subject to change at any time by the countries that have signed them. Therefore changes in regimes, government types or controlling parties could potentially affect any trade agreements.

Here are a few more important treaties that could affect your company abroad:

- The North American Free Trade Agreement (NAFTA) creates a trading bloc between the United States, Canada and Mexico, somewhat like the European Union.

- The Kyoto Protocol is an international agreement linked to the United Nations Framework Convention on Climate Change. It sets binding international emission reduction targets.

- The Patent Law Treaty is designed to streamline, harmonize and simplify the formal requirements set by national or regional patent offices in relation to applying for and maintaining patents.

These or other treaties may have specific effects on your business model and/or profitability. You will need to do your homework and perhaps consult the appropriate professionals in relation to your business. Note: In addition to attorneys and tax advisors, there are businesses and consultants who specialize in facilitating international trade.

Protection and free trade

There is an ongoing source of conflict related to international trade agreements. The competing positions are the protection of special industries by the industrialized countries vs. support for completely free trade by the developing nations. The primary industries involved here are agriculture and new technology. The developing countries want to protect their domestic agriculture sector through subsidies and tariffs to ensure that their countries will have enough food in the event of a famine or war. The developing countries are pushing for free trade on agriculture because that is a sector in which a developing nation could immediately compete, based on available land and cheap labor.

These conflicts continue into new or high tech industries which the political decision makers view as a future source of income or power. Such industries, e.g., computers or solar power, are often heavily subsidized by governments to ensure they grow within that country, even if they are not profitable. The heavy subsidies make it impossible for developing nations to compete in these sectors.

International business is a very real possibility for many businesses, even tiny start-ups, given today's globalized market. There is a lot to learn and consider, but by taking the time to think about it and factor it into your business plan, you will be better prepared to identify and develop opportunities in the long run.

S.G. and M.R.M.

Tariffs and Quotas and Trade, Oh My!

*Just the basics, so you can see
if you need to dig deeper.*

TO MANY ENTREPRENEURS, even those exploring international business, tariffs and quotas are subjects they skim past in the news. And in fact, their goods may not be affected by them. But it's smart to be informed, and you may in fact be affected. So here's your starter course.

What is a tariff?

It's a tax or a fee placed on the import or export of goods. Today, tariffs are heavily debated in various economic theories, with the arguments focusing, as ever, on protectionism vs. free trade. Tariffs have a strong connection with various political movements and have been very controversial throughout history. Well-known examples of tariffs include the British trade restrictions which led to the Boston Tea Party and sparked the American Revolution in the 18th Century, and the U.S.'s Smoot-Hawely Tariff Act, which significantly increased tarrifs just as the Great Depression of the 1930s was beginning. This Tariff sparked immediate retaliatory tariffs by most of the country's trading partners and is widely believed to have significantly contributed to the severity and length of the Depression.

Since World War II, the general view of free trade has been more positive and tariffs have been steadily reduced, playing a smaller role in international business and fiscal policy. However, there are still some significant tariffs in place on items like paper clips, canned tuna, sneakers, peanuts, tires and steel.

Countries use tariffs to protect a particular industry and to raise revenue. The government may decide to protect a specific industry because it is a newly established or developing industry (in the U.S., think of renewable energy technologies); it is an inefficient but critical industry (steel, agriculture); or because foreign companies are "dumping" in the industry, meaning that the foreign companies are flooding the market with below-market-value priced products with the intention of monopolizing the industry. The added cost to an import will make it easier for domestic products to compete and the added cost to an export will make it more likely that the good is not exported to that location.

Tariffs can be charged as a percentage of value or as a flat fee based on quantity. The revenues from the tariff go directly to the government. At one time this was the largest source of income for the U.S. federal government.

What is a quota?

Quotas are another economic government control measure used primarily to protect domestic producers and industries. Quotas are set by the government and specify an exact quantity of a particular good that may be exported or imported. They are a strongly protectionist control measure and are viewed as potentially harmful to a free-market economy, as they do not allow for any competition from foreign products and result in higher prices to consumers. Quotas are also called "non-tariff trade barriers". The history of trade quotas is very similar to that of tariffs—a popular, but controversial fiscal tool whose use has declined significantly after World War II.

There are a number of key industries in the U.S. that still have substantially limiting and controversial quotas in place. Those industries include sugar, tobacco, cotton, beef, anchovies, olives, Mandarin oranges and brooms. Other countries protect other industries, so check on their positions.

Fortunately, unless you are in a specifically regulated industry, the current tariffs and quotas should have very little effect on your business planning. If you are in one of those particular industries, then you will need to forecast any changes in trade policy in order to position your business for success.

M.R.M.

Immigration Issues

This area is fairly complex, so consider getting
an attorney's input if issues arise.

EACH COUNTRY HAS ITS OWN RULES, regulations and laws that cover immigration and related issues. These regulations will most often be at the national and international level and enforced by national-level agencies. Sometimes there are regional regulations as well.

While each jurisdiction is unique, there are some broad categories of immigration issues that especially impact businesses: illegal immigrants, asylum seekers or refugees, guest workers, and residents and tourists.

In most large countries there is a significant **illegal immigrant** population. Illegal immigrants are people who have entered the local region in violation of the controlling immigration laws of either the local region or their region of origin. Depending on the jurisdiction, illegal immigration may or may not actually constitute a crime. Each jurisdiction has unique standards of enforcement.

Illegal immigrants may be able to switch to a legal immigration status. Employing or doing business with illegal immigrants should be considered as a business decision after evaluating the penalties and benefits under your local laws and the market conditions. There is no universal answer.

Asylum seekers or refugees are people seeking refuge in the local region, outside of their home region or country, because of persecution, fear, war or other social upheaval. They may hope to stay short term, long term or permanently. There are international treaties and United Nations Conventions related to the definition and treatment of refugees. Generally speaking, upon arrival in the local region, the refugee must apply for asylum based on the above reasons. If the application is approved, she will be granted legal status in the local region, based on her circumstances.

Guest programs include guest workers and students. Some countries rely very heavily on guest worker programs to supplement their workforces. Guest worker programs are often controversial, as standards regarding the rights of guest workers and students while in the local region are not evenly enforced. International students and study abroad programs are also very common in our globalized world.

Guest worker status is a legal immigration designation given to foreign workers who temporarily work and live in the local region. Both the qualifications and the difficulty in acquiring this status change often and by jurisdiction. Usually guest-worker status is given to high-skill positions or to areas with an extreme shortage of available labor.

Student programs are similar in that they allow a legal immigration status for a certain period while the student participates in continuing education. If a student remains beyond the term specified, his status could change to being an illegal immigrant.

Almost all countries have immigration provisions dealing with **residents and tourists**. Residents are non-citizens who have been granted permission to live in the local region indefinitely. Individual jurisdictions may have ongoing requirements to seek citizenship or to contribute to the economy in some way. In countries already associated as trading partners, such as the European Union, the requirements are significantly easier.

Tourists are major economic driver and source of revenues for certain regions. Each jurisdiction will have individual requirements for documentation, length of stay, removal of goods and more. Generally speaking, tourism is encouraged but regulated.

M.R.M.

Immigration: Opportunities and Challenges

Talent, energy—and potential customers—
are moving around as never before.

WHAT IS IMMIGRATION? It's people moving into and settling in a non-native country or region. That movement can be international, regional or even local. Nowadays, practically all businesses have some experience with immigration and its effects on the workplace.

All over the world, immigration is an extremely complex, often controversial topic. It may be welcomed or opposed by the local population and represent dreams-come-true or nightmares for the immigrant. Immigration is a source of population growth and cultural change, but also of concern and conflict.

Factors that encourage immigration include open or porous borders, better opportunities, cheap land, rumors of instant wealth, higher pay, family reunification, better social welfare, better schools, political freedoms or religious callings. In countries generally considered to be economically open, immigrants often make up an extremely large percentage of the small-business community, perhaps because it may be easier to start a little business than to find work as an employee, or because entrepreneurial opportunity is what attracted the immigrant in the first place.

As globalization and international business shrink our planet every day, the ease with which people may move throughout the world in search of better opportunities is rising. This has caused immigration and closely related issues to be on the forefront of the political debates in most countries or regions. The exact issues vary greatly, depending on the location, but as a businessperson you should be aware of all of the political trends or pressures in all of the areas that your business operates. These political movements could include separatist movements, civil unrest, cultural conflicts, and restrictive or open immigration policies.

Looking for opportunities

People from elsewhere are very likely settling in your area now. They may come as political refugees, as workers seeking better opportunities, as invited members of a thriving ethnic community, as migrant workers, as investors, etc. They may prefer to preserve their own culture or choose to assimilate and adopt the local culture.

As immigrants interact with your business, their legal status could present both opportunities and legal issues for you, due to employment, taxation or other regulations. Seasonal immigration patterns could have significant practical effects on business as well.

Local patterns could include the development and growth of an immigrant community with a strong cultural identification. This could create or eliminate a market or source of labor and talent for your business's services or products. You need to know the answers to questions like these:

- Are these communities growing or shrinking?

- Are they integrating with surrounding and local cultures?

- Do they bring particular assets or interests you can tap for your business's growth?

- Are you part of this community? Can you develop connections, if not?

- Are there steps your business could take to capture this market for your goods or services, or tap its human resources for your workplace?

- Are there language differences or barriers you need to be aware of?

- Are there charitable or humanitarian things your business can do with or for the immigrants?

Often, simple small steps can make all the difference. For example, do you have your menu or website translated into the immigrants' language? (And by the way, do you take non-native speakers' needs into account in your company's documents, from internal policy manuals to signage in your shops for non-native speaking tourists, etc.?) Do you observe cultural distinctions or holidays that your immigrant colleagues observe? Finally, given the share of your target market that this particular community makes up, are there any competitors better poised to capture the market?

Seasonal migrations and "gold rushes"

Seasonal migrations can also affect businesses on many levels. These migratory patterns often can have significant ramifications for employees, consumers and others. Migratory workers usually follow peak labor needs in agriculture, fisheries, and in other sectors with defined planting, processing or harvest seasons. As many farmers have learned the hard way, a significant event affecting one crop can have a major impact on the migration patterns of workers, and consequently the farmers' costs and ability to effectively bring their crop to market.

From time to time around the world, a resource is discovered or a region or city starts a huge construction project, and these things attract workers as well. Your business might be on the fringe of all the frantic activity. It might gain or lose from the surge.

Emigration

Think of emigration as immigration, but viewed from the immigrant's original home base, with a focus on the loss of those who go away. Emigrants are those who leave a homeland or region. Their departures affect many regions and countries throughout the world.

Common examples include the brain drain, where educated and professional individuals study and then stay abroad, or go abroad after studies and create talent and knowledge shortages back home. Or the mass emigrations we've witnessed, away from rural and agricultural areas to urban economies worldwide, leaving not only no workers, but also no heirs for the family farms. These trends can cause costs of products to rise and fall, and ditto for business opportunities. Factors that generally push people to leave an area include natural disasters (drought, monsoon, volcanic eruption), high unemployment, lack of rights, land shortages, resource depletion, oppressive conditions or persecution, warfare, famine or expulsion.

What does this mean for my business?

Good question. Immigration patterns may have deep, far-reaching effects on your business. They could come in the form of economic, social, political, health, crime, environmental, educational or local attitude effects.

Economic effects are often the most apparent in the business context. Does this immigrant population provide a new market or workers for your business? Will it increase or decrease your costs? What does it mean for your revenues and profits?

Social effects are influenced by the prevailing social norms of both the local population and the immigrant population. Sometimes there is resistance and even opposition to immigration by local populations; but other times, strong preferences for immigrants dominate. Resistance can take the form of general opposition, racism or xenophobia. Preferences range from hiring British-accented telephone receptionists in locations outside the United Kingdom where their accent lends a feeling of "class" to the operation, to hiring mine workers willing to do hard labor for low wages.

Political effects are evident in your daily news. All the issues we touch on in this section are capable of generating tremendous political change, policy review, and heated discussion, if not street warfare. Virtually every business today is affected by immigration in some way.

Health concerns of immigration include the actual health of a population, the customs of a particular group and their impact on immigrants' health, their access to local health care and their actual or potential exposure to disease. Health issues directly correlate to immigrants' ability to look for immediate employment or their need for certain services. What access to health care services does your new immigrant worker have? Could that influence his ability to recover from illness and return to work?

Crime and corruption may occur, and affect your business, when immigration is prevalent. When people are displaced, they can become easy prey for criminals or exploiters. Immigrants might target other immigrants or local people, and local people might target immigrants. On the other hand, some immigrant communities have a much lower incidence of crime than the general population. This could be due to cultural norms or the close-knit nature of the group.

Also you should consider the **cultural norms of business** held by different groups. In some cultures it is considered rude to negotiate or to talk business without first discussing social matters like children and families. Others expect spirited give and take on pricing, and paying an initial asking price is never an option. Bribes or tips for good service are required in some cultures and never given in others. These norms tend to migrate along with people, so as you interact in business with immigrant counterparts, be aware of the norms that are in play.

The environmental concerns of immigration include the exploitation of all available resources for use vs. conservation, as well as overloads on public services when immigrant groups arrive *en masse* in an area. And people of different origins may have different standards regarding environmentally sound practices. Newcomers used to keeping and slaughtering chickens in the back yard may conflict with local ordinances. These issues often have long-term effects on the local environment and/or public opinion towards particular populations.

Educational considerations include the current language skills and education level of the immigrant population (and therefore your consumers or employees), their access to further education, and finally the long-term educational opportunities for subsequent generations. The current level is the most immediate concern for your business. If immigrants are your consumers, then you need to consider their language skills and education level when planning where and how you advertise, what you say on your packaging, etc. If you tap the group for workers, you need to consider language and education levels and adjust them in your hiring, training, employment and managing practices.

Ongoing education is another factor you should consider in developing immigrant workers' productivity and value. Supporting education at home is important too. Generally speaking, if your company's practices value education, and for example offer flex-time scheduling to allow workers to attend school or be involved in their children's school activities, everybody benefits. Cultures that value childhood education tend to be more stable.

Building a plan

The local attitudes towards immigration and immigrant groups should be factored into your business planning. In our globalized world, some form of this issue is near the top of the political debate in most regions. Whether it is related to the open or restrictive nature of the general policy, the legal status of protectionist measures of certain industries, or other issues, it is a heated debate. Your decision as a business owner to interact with immigrants could have short- and long-term effects on your business operations and should be reviewed carefully and periodically.

The economic or other conditions of the home country should also be considered in planning in relation to immigrant populations. For instance, the resolution of a home country conflict could lead to a mass movement back to the home region and a loss of employees or consumers for your business. Or a shift in the currency exchange rate back home could be a significant factor in determining what wage an immigrant may need to earn as your employee.

Finally, it's important to remember that many immigrants have a specific goals that motivate them: to get an education and move back home, to earn money and send it home, to save enough money to move the family to their location or to attain local citizenship. These goals should also be considered in your business planning. You can't predict the future, but you can consider it in advance.

M.R.M.

Afterword:
Where to Go from Here?

IT MAY BE SAFE TO ASSUME that if you've just finished reading this book, you are one of two types of individuals. The *curious* reader may have been interested in learning how a potentially successful business could be envisioned, created and then finally launched to compete in the marketplace. For curious readers, these pages may have even sparked your imagination about becoming an entrepreneur one day. Curious readers have always shown interest in educating and informing themselves on a new topic and enhancing their knowledgebase while doing so.

The *serious* reader may have chosen to read our book because he or she may have already decided to toss a hat in the ring and become an entrepreneur. Or perhaps, you've launched your business, and now additional tools, expert guidance, and real-world examples of business law are vital to your success. A serious reader never stops perusing every possible source for innovative ideas, the next greatest trend, or even a leg up on the competition.

Curious or serious, we hope that everyone who has read this fifth volume of our series found the material worthy of your time. Regardless of how or why you found us, we are glad you did.

For the three of us who founded the Expert Business Advice website, and for Mark Moon in his legal practice, the philosophy is simple:

- Create material of substance and value that can continue to be expanded indefinitely for the benefit of the reader, the customer, and the business professional
- Deliver the best possible ideas, resources and guidance to those who seek it
- Take ownership of our work, stand by it, and be proud of it

Developing this material from several points of view and delivering it to people from diverse backgrounds and with multiple levels of experience was crucial for us. In fact, it was the only way we could imagine doing it.

Simply put, our goal with this series shares the same vision as Expert Business Advice's slogan: "Experts Create | We Deliver | You Apply."

The way forward begins here…

Acknowledgements

WE HAVE A LOT OF THANKS TO GIVE.

Scott Girard wishes to thank his wife Kellin, his co-authors, his parents, the Girard Family, the Conway Family, the Edwards Family, the Seaman Family, the Warren Family (keep up the writing, Lea), the O'Keefe Family, the Thomas Family, the Price Family, everyone at Pinpoint Holdings Group, Barbara Stephens, Jack Chambless, Mary-Jo Tracy, Sandra McMonagle, Diane Orsini, Nathan Holic, Peter Telep, Pat Rushin, and the Seminole Battalion.

Mike O'Keefe wishes to thank his parents Tim and Gaye O'Keefe, his co-authors, Jamie, Kimberly Rupert, the O'Keefe Family, the Goldsberry Family, the Roy Family, the Hubert Family, the Murat Family, the Grant Family, the Girard Family, the Price Family, the Holycross Family, the most inspiring professor Jack Chambless, his two favorite authors Clive Cussler and Timothy Ferriss, and those individuals in Argentina (for making sure there is always Malbec on the table).

Marc Price wishes to thank his wife Dawn; his co-authors; his mom Lynda; the Price Family; the O'Bryan Family; the Smith Family; Jean Hughes; the O'Keefe Family; the Girard Family; Mike Schiano; David Wittschen and Family; Kurt Ardaman; Axum Coffee in Winter Garden, Florida; and his life-long mentor, Howard Satin.

Mark Moon wishes to thank his wife, Marguerite, for sticking with him and for being his pillar of strength; he will always love her, truly, madly and deeply. He would like to thank their entire family for being so understanding of everything he does. He would like to thank his professional mentors for making him the practitioner he is today, especially Paul Tabio, Lee-Ford Tritt, Dennis A. Calfee, Richard Gallant, Vaughn Brown, Julio Acosta, Eugene Meisenheimer, Paul McGarr and Anne Nymark. Mark would like to thank the Moon Law Group team who make the dream work every day: Donna Casavant, Rhonda Orlosky, Melissa McCoy, Katrina Spriet, Mary Huntsman, Mai Vu and Mark Sodhi. He would like to thank his peers, who continue to inspire and drive him: Brian McKenzie, Adam Sudbury, Josh Law, Ingrid Hooglander, Joryn Jenkins, Brad Goodwin, Jasen Pask, Josh Walker, Scott Girard, Matthew Tebow, Justin Egan and Tad Schnaufer. Finally, Mark would like to thank all of his past, present and future clients for providing him the opportunity to do what he loves to do on a daily basis.

The authors would collectively like to thank Kathe Grooms and everyone at Nova Vista Publishing, everyone at Expert Business Advice, Jon Collier, and the Van Beekum Family: Dave, Melissa and the Sugar Gliders.

Glossary

Note: We are pleased that this book is being marketed worldwide. However, that means that you may encounter legal terms and practices that differ from some that we commonly use. We suggest that if you need help, you visit the many web sites that provide simple definitions and short, informative articles for extra help.

Accountant	One who is trained and qualified in the practice of accounting or who is in charge of public or private accounts.
Accounting	The systematic recording, reporting and analysis of the financial transactions of a business or government.
Accredited Investor	A term defined by various countries' securities laws that characterizes investors permitted to invest in certain types of higher risk investments including seed money, limited partnerships, hedge funds, private placements, and angel investor networks. The term generally includes wealthy individuals and financially-oriented organizations such as banks, insurance companies, significant charities, some corporations, endowments, and retirement plans.
Acquisitions	Acquiring control of a business, called a target, by stock purchase or exchange, either hostile or friendly. Also called a takeover.
Acumen	Keenness and swiftness in understanding and dealing with a business situation in a manner that is likely to lead to a good outcome.
Advertising	A form of communication used to encourage or motivate an audience to take or continue to take some new action. Most commonly, the desired result is to guide consumer behavior regarding a commercial offering.
Agency Law	An aspect of legal practice that involves one person receiving legal authority to act for another. This may include contractual, quasi-contractual and non-contractual fiduciary relationships.
Analytics	The application of computer technology, operational research, and statistics to alleviate problems in business and industry.
Anchor Tenant	The business or individual who is serving as the primary draw to a commercial property.
Angel Investor	An individual who provides funding to one or more start-up companies. The individual is usually affluent or has a personal interest in the success of the venture. Such investments are distinguished by high levels of risk and a potentially large return on investment.

Arbitration	See *Mediation and Arbitration.*
Balance Sheet	A quantitative synopsis of a company's financial condition at a specific point in time, including assets, liabilities and net worth. The first part of a balance sheet illustrates all the productive assets a company owns, and the second part shows all the financing methods (such as liabilities and shareholders' equity). Also called a statement of condition.
Ball-Park Figure	A figure given as an estimated value based on information available. Also called a ball park estimate.
Bid Bond	A bond purchased by a business or individual when bidding on a large project or sale, in order to demonstrate that sufficient funding exists to complete the transaction if the bidder is selected. The bond guarantees that the bidder will not be prevented from fulfilling the contract by availability by lack of funding.
Bilateral Contract	A reciprocal agreement between two parties where each promises to perform (or not perform) act in exchange for the other party's act. See *Unilateral Contract.*
Board of Directors	Individuals elected by a business's shareholders to oversee the management of the business.
Bonding Company	A financial entity, most commonly an insurance company, which assumes the risk of a surety bond obligee by guaranteeing payment on the bond in the event of a default or a failure of the obligee to perform its contracted services.
Bookkeeping	The systematic transcription of a business's financial transactions.
Bottom Line	The amount left after taxes, interest, depreciation, and other expenses are subtracted from gross sales. Also called net earnings, net income, or net profit.
Boundaries	A theoretical or literal line that marks the limits of an area or agreement; a dividing line.
Brainstorming	A group creativity technique in which members spontaneously and freely generate a list of ideas to address a specific opportunity or problem.
Brain-Trust Equity	Equity that is accepted or earned through an individual's contribution of information, ideas, or concepts to the strategic growth, development or direction of a company and its products, services or organizational structure.
Brand	An identifying symbol, word, phrase or mark that identifies and distinguishes a product or business from its competitors.
Branding	The act of identifying a product or business and distinguishing it from its competitors by utilizing unique symbols, words, or marks.

Brick-and-Mortar Business	A description of a company or portion of a company with a physical presence, as opposed to one that exists only virtually, on the Internet.
Budget	An itemized prediction of an individual's or business's income and expenses expected for some period in the future.
Budget Deficit	The amount by which a business or individual's spending exceeds its income over a specific period of time.
Business	A commercial activity engaged in as a means of occupation or income, or an entity which engages in such activities.
Business Consultant	An individual or company that provides advising, analyzing, monitoring, training, reviewing or reporting services to commercial clients.
Business Dissolution	The process by which a company (or part of a company) is brought to an end. Sometimes called winding down a business.
Business License	Permits issued by government agencies that grant individuals or companies the right to conduct business within the government's geographical jurisdiction. It is the authorization to start a new business issued by the local government.
Business Model	A description of the operations of a business including the segments of the business; its functions, roles and relationships; and the revenues and expenses that the business generates.
Business Operations	Ongoing recurring activities involved in running a business in order to generate value for its stakeholders.
Business Plan	A document prepared by a company's management, or by a consultant on their behalf, that details the past, present, and future of the company, usually for the purpose of attracting capital investment.
Business Taxes	Taxes owed and paid by a corporate entity.
Buyout	The purchase or acquisition of controlling interest in one corporation by another corporation, in order to take over assets and/or operations.
Bylaws	A set of rules made by a business to control the actions of its members.
C-Corporation	A business which, unlike a partnership, is a completely separate entity from its owners. Also called a C-Corp.
Capital	1. Cash or goods used to produce income either by investing in a business or a different income property.
	2. The net worth of a company; that is, the amount by which its assets exceed its liabilities.
	3. The money, property, and other valuables which collectively represent the value of an individual or business.

Capital Expenditure	Money spent to acquire or enhance physical assets such as buildings and machinery. Also called capital spending or capital expense.
Capital Requirements	The amount of cash a business needs for its normal operations.
Cash Capital Disbursement	The repaying of a debt or expense.
Cash Flow Positive	The situation when income exceeds liabilities.
Cash Flow Statement	A summary of a business's cash flow over a given period of time.
Class A Office Space	These buildings represent the highest quality buildings available. They are generally the most attractive buildings with the best construction, and possess high quality building infrastructure. Class A buildings also are well-located, have good access, and are managed by professionals.
Class B Office Space	One notch down from Class A quality, Class B buildings are generally a little older, but are still well-managed. Often, value-added investors target these buildings as investments, since well-located Class B buildings can be returned to their Class A status through renovation such as façade and common area improvements.
Collateral	Assets pledged by a borrower to secure a loan or other credit, and subject to seizure in the event of default. Also called security.
Company Description	The third section of a business plan. A brief synopsis that describes how all of the different components in a business work together.
Competitor	A business or person that provides similar products or services.
Confidentiality	The state of being secret; in business, it has to do with keeping information in the hands of those who are trusted not to share it.
Contingency Plan	A plan devised for an outcome other than the one in the expected plan.
Contract	A legally binding agreement.
Controlling Interest	The ownership of a majority of a company's voting stock; or a significant fraction, even if less than the majority, if the rest of the shares are not actively voted.
Convertible Debt	Security which can be converted for a specified amount of another, related security, at the option of the issuer and/or the holder. Also called convertible.
Copyright	The exclusive right to produce and dispose of copies of a literary, musical, or artistic work.
Corp.	The abbreviation for *corporation*.
Corporate Attorney	An attorney who specializes in business law.

Corporation	The most common form of business organization, which is given many legal rights as an entity separate from its owners. This form of business is characterized by the limited liability of its owners, the issuance of shares of easily transferable stock, and existence as a going concern.
Credentials	A tangible representation of qualification, competence, or authority issued to an individual by a third party with a relevant authority or assumed competence to do so.
Credit	The borrowing ability of an individual or company.
Credit History	A record of an individual's or company's past borrowing and repaying behavior.
Credit Report	A report comprised of detailed information on a person's credit history.
Credit Score	A numerically represented measure of credit risk calculated from a credit report using a standardized formula.
Creditworthiness	A creditor's measure of an individual's or company's ability to meet debt responsibilities.
Curriculum Vitae	A résumé; an overview of a person's experience and other qualifications. Also called a CV.
Customer Service	The supply of service to customers before, during and after a purchase.
Damages	A monetary award paid to a person as compensation for injury or loss. See also *Equitable Relief*.
Deadline	The date by which something has to be accomplished.
Debt	An amount owed to a person or organization for funds borrowed.
Debt Financing	Financing by selling bonds, bills or notes to individuals or businesses.
Debt Retirement	The repayment of a debt.
Debt-to-Income Ratio	A figure that calculates how much income is spent repaying debts.
Deduction	An expense subtracted from adjusted gross income when calculating taxable income. Also called tax deduction.
Defendant	A party sued or accused in a court of law.
Delta	Balance. For example, when demand equals supply. Also called equilibrium. Can also mean degree of change, or change itself.
Demographics	Data on socioeconomic groups, e.g., age, income, sex, education, occupation, etc., often used to study or profile a target market.
Design Patent	A patent issued on the ornamental design of a functional item.

Disclaimer   A statement made to remove oneself from responsibility. Also called hedge clause.

Dividend   A taxable cash award declared by a company's board of directors and given to its shareholders out of the company's current or retained earnings, usually quarterly. Also used as a slang term to mean reward.

Double Taxation   Taxation of the same income at two levels. One common example is taxation of earnings at the personal income level and then again at the sales level.

Economics   The study of how the forces of supply and demand assign scarce resources.

Economy   Activities related to the production and distribution of goods and services in a specific geographic region.

Employment Agreement A contract between an employer and employee.

Entrepreneur   An individual who starts his or her own business.

EPO   Acronym for European Patent Office.

Equitable Relief   A court-granted remedy that requires a party to act or abstain from performing a particular act, not involving money. See also *Damages*.

Equity   Ownership interest in a business in the form of common stock or preferred stock.

Equity Financing   Financing a business by selling common or preferred stock to investors.

Escalator Clause   A clause in a contract that guarantees a change in the basic, agreed price under certain conditions.

Establishments   Organizations.

European Patent Office One of the two offices of the European Patent Organization. The other is the Administrative Council.

Expense   Any cost of conducting business.

Expense Report   A document that contains all the expenses that a business has incurred as a result of the business's operation.

Fair Isaac Corporation A publicly traded company that provides analytics and decision making services, including credit scoring, intended to help financial services companies make complex, high-volume decisions.

Farming Out   A slang term for outsourcing, in which organizations hire vendors to perform duties the organizations choose not to do themselves in-house.

FICO   Acronym for Fair Isaac Corporation.

Financial Adviser   A person or organization employed by a business or mutual fund to manage assets or provide investment advice.

Financials	Documents related to finance.
Financing	Providing the necessary monetary capital.
Fixed Expense	An expense that does not change depending on production or sales levels, such as rent, property tax, insurance, or interest expense. Also called fixed cost.
Forfeiture	The act of forfeiting.
Franchise	A form of business organization in which a company which already has a successful product or service (the franchisor) enters into a continuing contractual agreement with other businesses (franchisees) operating under the franchisor's trade name, usually with the franchisor's guidance, in exchange for a fee.
Franchising	The practice of licensing a successful business model.
Fulfillment	Accomplishment. Also can mean storing, order processing and shipment of goods.
Funding Request	A request for funding.
General Partner	A partner with unlimited legal obligation for the debts and liabilities of a partnership.
Goods and Services Taxes (GST)	A tax on the amount of added value supplied by an entity which then passes it on to another level of sale. That value is subtracted from the GST the entity paid out in a given period. Example: You sell your product to a retailer. The retailer adds GST and the consumer pays the total for the goods plus GST it. You get to deduct what you paid from your GST taxes due.
Grant	Funds disbursed by the grantor to a recipient.
Gross Margin	A measure of profitability, often shortened to GM. To calculate divide Gross Income by Net Sales, and express it as a percentage. For example, a widget sells for $5 and costs $3 to make.
	$5 (Net Sales) - $3 (Cost of Goods) = $2 (Gross Income).
	Then $2 \div 5 = 0.4$, which expressed as a percentage is 40% Gross Margin.
Growth Rate	A measure of financial growth.
Growth Strategy	A plan of action based on investing in companies and sectors which are growing faster than their peers. Also can mean an organization's plan for increasing, expanding, and otherwise getting bigger.
GST	See *Goods and Services Taxes.*
Hardware	A general term for equipment that can be touched. In business, *hardware* most commonly refers to computer hardware; laptops, desktops, monitors, etc. In general, computer software operates on computer hardware.

Home-Based Business	A small business that operates from the business owner's home. Also called a home business.
Immigration Law	National government policies which control immigration to their country.
Inc.	Abbreviation for incorporated.
Income	Revenues minus cost of sales, operating expenses, and taxes, over a given period of time.
Income Statement	A document illustrating sales, expenses, and net profit for a given period.
Incorporated	A business that has been formed into a legal corporation by completing the required procedures.
Indemnity Bond	An insurance bond used as an additional measure of security to cover loan amounts, worth about 75 percent of the value of the property. This bond protects lenders from loss, in the event that the borrower defaults on the loan.
Industry Standard	A practice accepted as convention by industry members, either through formal agreement or through emulation of best practices established by industry leaders.
Inheritance Taxes	A tax imposed on someone who inherits property or money.
Initial Public Offering	The initial sale of stock by a company to the public.
Insolvency	Being unable to pay debts.
Intellectual Property (IP)	Creations of the mind.
Interest	The return earned on an investment.
Internal Revenue Service	The federal agency of the United States responsible for administering and enforcing the U.S. Treasury Department's revenue laws, through the assessment and collection of taxes, determination of pension plan qualification, and related activities.
International Securities Identifier Number	A exclusive international code which identifies a securities issue.
Internet	Commonly called a network of networks, the Internet is a global system of interconnected computer networks that use the standard Internet protocol suite to serve billions of users worldwide.
Internship	On-the-job training for college (or sometimes high school) students.
Interview	A discussion between two people where questions are asked by the interviewer in order to gather information from the interviewee. Often part of a hiring process.

Investment Banker	An individual who acts as an underwriter or agent for businesses and municipalities issuing securities.
Investment Group	A group of investors who pool some of their money and make joint investments. Also called an investment club.
Investor	An individual who commits monetary capital to investment products with the expectation of financial return.
IPO	Acronym for Initial Public Offering.
IRS	Acronym for Internal Revenue Service.
ISIN	Acronym for International Securities Identifier Number.
Keyman Insurance	Also called "Key Person Insurance", an insurance policy taken out by a company to compensate that company for losses that would arise from the death or extended incapacity of an important performer in the company.
Lawsuit	A civil action brought to a court of law for adjudication.
Leader	An individual who guides.
Legal Representation	An attorney. Also called a lawyer.
Lending Portfolio	A collection of investments all owned by the same person or organization.
Letter of Intent (LOI)	A written document that details the proposal or intentions of the writer.
Letter of Reference	A letter in which an employer, past or present, recommends someone for a new job. Also called a letter of recommendation.
Leveraged Buyout	The takeover of a company or controlling interest of a company (a buyout), involving a significant amount of borrowed (leveraged) money.
Liability	An obligation that legally commits an individual or company to settle a debt.
Licensing	Under defined conditions, the granting of permission to use intellectual property rights, such as trademarks, patents, or technology.
Limited Liability Company	A type of company, authorized only in certain business sectors, whose owners and managers receive the limited liability and tax benefits of an S-Corporation without having to conform to S-Corporation restrictions.
Limited Partner	A partner in a business whose liability is limited to the extent of the partner's share of the business's ownership.
Liquidation	The process by which a company dissolves or comes to an end.
Liquidity	The ability of an asset or property to be converted into cash quickly and without any price discount.

Litigation	The process of taking legal action to enforce a particular right.
LLC	Acronym for limited liability company.
Loan	An arrangement in which a lender gives monetary capital or property to a borrower, and the borrower agrees to return the property or repay the monetary capital, usually along with interest, at some future point in time.
Logo	A graphic mark or wordmark used by individuals or organizations to aid and promote instant public recognition.
LOI	See *Letter of Intent.*
Malpractice	Professional negligence, improper or illegal acts.
Mandate	A command or order.
Market Analysis	Research intended to predict the expectations of a market.
Marketing	The process by which products and services are announced and launched into the marketplace.
Marketplace	The area—actual, virtual or metaphorical—in which a market operates.
Market Share	The percentage of the total sales of a given type of product or service that is won by given company.
Media	Entities used to store and deliver information or data.
Mediation and Arbitration	The most common forms of dispute resolution to avoid litigation.
Memorandum of Agreement	A binding, yet somewhat informal, agreement that allows two or more parties to name key points in a relationship so they can proceed in their work together, pending a more formal contract.
Memorandum of Understanding	A bilateral or multilateral agreement between two or more parties that expresses an understanding of will between the parties which indicates an intended common line of action. May be binding or not binding.
Merger	A legal union between two or more businesses.
Middleman	Intermediary between two commercial entities, commonly a wholesaler or distributor who buys from a manufacturer and sells to a retailer or to consumer.
Misrepresentation	Providing a false or misleading account of something.
MOA	See *Memorandum of Agreement.*
Municipality	An administrative division that has corporate status and usually self-governing powers.
NDA	See *Non-Disclosure Agreement.*
Negligence	Failure to take reasonable care in doing something.
Network	An arrangement of connections.

Non-Compete Agreement	An agreement through which an employee contractually agrees not to enter into or start a similar profession or trade in competition against his or her current or former employer.
Non-Disclosure Agreement (NDA)	A contract between two or more parties that outlines confidential material, knowledge, or information that the parties wish to keep confidential from others.
Open Market	A market which is widely and generally accessible to all investors or consumers.
Operating Agreement	An agreement among key members of a company that governs the company's business, and the members' financial and managerial rights and duties.
Operating Expense	An expense arising in the normal course of running a business, such as manufacturing, advertising and sales.
OPEX	Acronym for operating expense.
Outsourcing	Work executed for a business by people other than the business's full-time employees.
Over-Saturated Market	In a market occupied by buyers and sellers, a market that is filled with sellers to the point that it negatively affects each seller's opportunity to make a significant profit. Also called a saturated market.
Owner-Operated	An organization that is operated in full or in majority by its owner.
Ownership Equity	The owner's share of the assets of a business.
Partners	Members of a partnership, either general or limited.
Partnership	A relationship of two or more entities, people or companies, conducting business for mutual benefit.
Passion	Intense emotion; used in business to identify positive dedication and engagement by someone with an idea, activity, role, etc.
Patent	The exclusive right, granted by the government, to use an invention or process for a given period of time, usually 14 years.
Payment Bond	A surety bond through which a contractor assures an owner that material and labor provided in the completion of a project will be fully paid for, and that no mechanics' liens will be filed against the owner.
Performance Bond	A bond issued to guarantee adequate and acceptable completion of a project by a contractor.
Permit	The legal authorization or physical item which grants someone permission to do something.
Personal Finances	One's private funds, property, possessions. The application of finance principles to the monetary decisions of a person or family.
Plaintiff	A party who brings a case against another in a court of law.
Principle	A rule or ethical standard.

Private Labeling   A retailer's name, as used on a product sold by the retailer but manufactured by another company.

Private Placement   The sale of shares directly to an institutional investor, such as a bank, mutual fund, insurance company, pension fund, or foundation.

Private Placement Disclaimer   A disclaimer that specifies that the sale of securities directly to an institutional investor, such as a bank, mutual fund, foundation, insurance company, etc. does not require Securities Exchange Commission (SEC) registration, provided that the securities are purchased for investment purchases only, not for resale.

Pro Forma   Description of financial statements that have one or more assumptions or hypothetical conditions built into the data. Often used with balance sheets and income statements when data is not available, to construct scenarios. One variety is called a Pro Forma Income Statement. Another is a Pro Forma Invoice.

Profit   The positive gain from an investment or business operation after deducting all expenses.

Promissory Note   A document signed by a borrower promising to repay a loan under agreed-upon terms. Also called a note.

Proof of Concept   Evidence from a market test or trial period that demonstrates that a business model or idea is feasible.

Publicity   Information that attracts attention to a business, product, person, or event.

Ratio Analysis   The study and interpretation of the relationships between various financial variables, used often by investors or lenders.

Reformation   Rewriting a contract to clarify or correct it.

Research   The process of acquiring and organizing information for the purpose of initiating, modifying or terminating a particular investment or group of investments.

Résumé   A brief written synopsis of an individual's education, work experience, and accomplishments, typically for the purposes of finding a job. Also called a curriculum vitae, or CV.

Retainer   A fee paid to someone in advance or on a regular basis to secure their services when required.

Revenue   The total amount of money received by an organization for goods or services provided during a certain time period. Sometimes called turnover.

Risk   The quantifiable probability of loss or less-than-expected returns.

S-Corporation   A corporate tax status choice (election), recognized in the U.S. by the Internal Revenue Service for most companies with 75 or fewer shareholders, which enables the company to enjoy the benefits of incorporation but be taxed as if it were a partnership. Also called Subchapter S Corporation, or S-Corp.

Sales	Total monetary amount collected for goods and services provided.
Sales Activity	The act of selling.
Sales Force	A group of people whose only corporate responsibility is to sell a company's products or services.
Sales Force Strategy	The strategic plan of a sales force to penetrate and have lasting impact on the market.
SBA	Acronym for the Small Business Administration in the US.
SBA Loan	A business loan issued by the US Small Business Administration.
Shareholder	One who owns shares of stock in a corporation or mutual fund. For corporations, along with the ownership comes a right to declared dividends and the right to vote on certain company matters, including the board of directors. Also called a stockholder.
Small Business Administration	A US Federal agency which offers loans to small businesses.
Social Media	Web-based and mobile technologies used to turn communication into interactive dialogue between organizations, communities, and individuals. They are ubiquitously accessible, and enabled by scalable communication techniques.
Socioeconomics	Referring to social and economic conditions, social classes and income groups.
Software	A accumulation of computer programs and related data that provides the instructions that tell a computer what to do and how to do it.
Sole Proprietorship	A company which is not registered with the state as a limited liability company or corporation and is a business structure in which an individual and his/her company are considered a single entity for tax and liability purposes.
Stakeholder	Anyone who is interested in or affected by something; one who could benefit from information about it. Not to be confused with shareholders.
Start-Up	1. The beginning of a new company or new product. 2. A new, usually small business that is just beginning its operations, especially a new business supported by venture capital and in a sector where new technologies are used.
Start-Up Capital	The initial stage in financing a new project, which is followed by several rounds of investment capital as the project gets under way
Statement of Cash Flows	A summary of a company's cash flow over a given period of time. Also called Cash Flow Statement.
Stock Symbol	Ticker symbol for a stock.
Strategy	A planned system of action.

Strengths	Actions a business accomplishes exceptionally or easily; assets.
Subsidy	Financial aid given by the government to individuals or groups.
Surety Bond	A bond issued by an entity on behalf of a second party, guaranteeing that the second party will fulfill an obligation or series of obligations to a third party. In the event that the obligations are not met, the third party can recover its losses via the bond.
Synopsis	A summary.
Takeover	Acquiring control of a corporation, called a target, by stock purchase or exchange, either hostile or friendly.
Target Market	The selection of a market that will be the most advantageous segment in which to offer a product or service. Also called a market target.
Tariff	A tax to be paid on imports or exports.
Tax Implications	Conditions or actions that can affect the amount of taxes payable.
Taxes	A fee levied (charged) by a government on a product, income, or activity.
Ticker	A scrolling display of current or recent security prices and/or volume.
Time Management	The act or process of planning and exercising conscious control over the amount of time spent on specific activities, especially to increase effectiveness, efficiency or productivity.
Tort	A civil wrongdoing that leads to civil legal liability.
Trademark	A distinctive name, symbol, motto, or design that legally identifies a company or its products and services, and sometimes prevents others from using identical or similar marks.
Trade Secret	A formula, process, system, tool, etc. which provides a company with a competitive advantage.
Trading Platform	Software provided by a stock broker in order to buy and sell shares in the stock market.
Treaty	A formally concluded and sanctioned agreement between two or more countries.
Trend Analysis	A comparative analysis of a company's financial ratios over time.
Trends	The current general direction of movement for prices or rates. Also, increasingly frequent or widespread behavior.
Trust	A confidence placed in someone by making that person the nominal owner of an estate to be held or used for the benefit of one or more others.
Underwriting	The procedure by which an underwriter brings a new security issue to the investing public in an offering. In such a case, the underwriter will guarantee a certain price for a certain number of securities to the party that is issuing the security. Thus, the issuer is secure that they will raise a certain minimum from the issue, while the underwriter bears the risk of the issue.

Unilateral Contract	A one-sided, legally binding agreement whereby one party promises to do, or refrain from doing, something. See *Bilateral Contract*.
United States Copyright Office	The US Government body that maintains records of copyright registration in the United States.
United States Patent and Trademark Office	An agency in the United States Department of Commerce that issues patents to inventors and businesses for their inventions, and trademark registration for product and intellectual property identification.
USCO	Acronym for United States Copyright Office.
USPTO	Acronym for United States Patent and Trademark Office.
Value Added Taxes (VAT)	See *Goods and Services Tax*. VAT is roughly the same as GST.
Variable Expense	A cost of labor, material or overhead that changes according to the change in the volume of production units. Combined with fixed costs, variable costs make up the total cost of production. Also called variable cost.
Venture Capitalist	An investor who engages in venture capital projects. Venture capitalists seek opportunities involving businesses that are growing or are in risky market segments, since these businesses generally have a harder time obtaining loans. Frequently called VCs.
Web-Based Business	A company that does most of its business on the Internet, usually through a website that uses the popular top-level domain, *.com*. Also called an Internet business, web business, dot-com company, or simply a dot-com.
Wholesale	The purchase of goods in quantity for resale purposes. Also called wholesale distribution.
Wholesale Distribution	See *wholesale*.
Workers' Compensation	A form of insurance providing wage replacement and medical benefits to employees injured at work. In exchange, employees agree not to sue their employer for negligence.
Working Capital	Current liabilities subtracted from current assets. Working capital measures the liquid assets a company has available to build its business.

Resources

ExpertBusinessAdvice.com

At **ExpertBusinessAdvice.com**, our goal is to become your complete resource for simple, easy-to-use business information and resources. Enjoy reading about techniques and processes necessary to develop and grow your business. **ExpertBusinessAdvice. com** offers an array of tools and resources to help you along the way by offering tutorials, downloadable templates, real-life examples, and customer support. You can even email us and a qualified member of our staff (yes, a real person!) will review your inquiry and get back to you. Now you can take charge of your professional growth and development, learn from others' success, and make a dramatic positive impact on your business. Learn the principles and practices that seasoned professionals use, at **ExpertBusinessAdvice.com,** for free!

THE WAY FORWARD BEGINS HERE...

Want to learn how to start a business? Are you looking for an additional income stream? No problem—we can get you started down the right path. Do you want to know how to plan, creating the necessary documents to obtain financing for your business? Maybe you just want to learn how experienced business leaders streamline financial models, maximize output, inspire managers, and incentivize employees, tapping the full range of resources available. Regardless of your needs, **ExpertBusinessAdvice. com** is here for you!

www.expertbusinessadvice.com

CRASH COURSE for ENTREPRENEURS

Many novice entrepreneurs have little more than a brilliant idea and a pocketful of ambition. They want to know *Now what?* This 12-title series tells *exactly what you must know*, in simple terms, using real-world examples. Each two-hour read walks you through a key aspect of being an entrepreneur and gives practical, seasoned, reader-friendly advice.

Whether your dream business is dog walking or high-tech invention, home-based or web-based, these books will save you time and trouble as you set up and run your new company. Collectively, these three young Florida-based serial entrepreneurs have successfully started seventeen new companies across a broad range of sectors and frameworks, including finance, international sourcing, medical products, innovative dot-com initiatives, and traditional brick-and-mortar companies.

A Crash Course for Entrepreneurs—From Expert Business Advice

Starting a Business – Everything you need to build a new business, starting from scratch.

Sales and Marketing – Solid guidance on successfully developing and promoting your business and its brand.

Managing Your Business – Proven techniques in managing employees and guiding your business in the right direction.

Business Finance Basics – Tax tips, funding resources, money management, basic accounting, and more!

Business Law Basics – A must-know overview on types of businesses, risks and liabilities, required documents, regulatory requirements, and the role of a business attorney. *Co-Author: Mark R. Moon, Esq.*

International Business – The world is a big place filled with billions of potential partners and customers. This guide offers tips to reach them all.

Business Plans – The quality of thinking and planning in your business plan is critical to your start-up's success. Learn how to build a great one and see samples of excellence.

Time and Efficiency – Wheel-spinning is the most destructive force in business. Make the most of your time to maximize income and motivate employees.

Franchising – A how-to guide for buying and running a franchise business.

Supplemental Income – Can't commit full time? No problem! Here's how to make extra money in your spare time.

Social Media – This rapidly-growing networking and advertising medium is changing the world. Here's how to use it to grow your business.

Web-Based Business – The biggest, most valuable companies out there today are Internet businesses. Here's why, and how you can build one yourself.

Paperback and eBook format available. 160 or 192 pages, 6 ½" × 9" (16.5 × 23 cm), US$18.95, with extensive glossary and index.

expertbusinessadvice.com   moonlawgroup.com   novavistapub.com

Index

Tip: We suggest you check the Glossary for definitions related to items in this Index.

About the Authors

Scott L. Girard, Jr.

Editor-in-Chief, Expert Business Advice, LLC
Email: scott@expertbusinessadvice.com

Before joining Expert Business Advice, Scott was Executive Vice President of Pinpoint Holdings Group, Inc., where he directed multiple marketing and advertising initiatives. Scott was a key player for the Group, negotiating and facilitating the sourcing logistics for the commercial lighting industry division, which supplied clients such as Gaylord Palms, Ritz Carlton, Marriott, Mohegan Sun, and Isle of Capri with large-scale lighting solutions. His vision and work were also pivotal in the growth and development of Bracemasters International, LLC.

Scott has degrees in Business Administration and English Writing and is a published contributor to various periodicals on the topics of economics and politics. He is also a co-author and series editor of A Crash Course for Entrepreneurs book series. A graduate of the United States Army Officer Candidate School and the Infantry Officer Basic Course, Scott is a combat veteran, having served in Iraq, Afghanistan, Kuwait and Qatar in support of Operation Iraqi Freedom, Operation Enduring Freedom, and Operation New Dawn.

Originally from Glendale, California, Scott now lives in St. Petersburg, Florida with his wife and son. Scott is a regular contributor to www.expertbusinessadvice.com. His side projects include a collection of short stories and scripts for two feature films. His motto: "Words have meaning."

Michael F. O'Keefe

Chief Executive Officer, Expert Business Advice, LLC
Email: mike@expertbusinessadvice.com

In 2004, Michael founded O'Keefe Motor Sports, Inc. (OMS Superstore), eventually growing it into one of the largest databases of aftermarket automotive components available on the web. Currently, aside from his position at Expert Business

Advice, LLC, Michael is the President of Pinpoint Holdings Group, Inc. and the Vice President of Marketing for Bracemasters International, LLC.

At Pinpoint Holdings Group, Inc., Michael focuses on strategically building a diverse portfolio of assets including technology, biomedical and traditional brick-and-mortar companies, as well as commercial and residential real estate. He also played a key role in facilitating the logistics of the commercial lighting branch of the company, bridging the gap between Pinpoint's office in Wuxi, China, and their commercial clients.

Recently, Michael's passion and talents for contemporary business techniques and practices were demonstrated in the exponential growth of Bracemasters International, LLC. Michael developed dynamic marketing campaigns, web-based marketing strategies, and e-Commerce initiatives resulting in Bracemasters' website viewership growing by 17,000 percent in just under two years and its annual revenues growing by over 100 percent. Michael's talent, leadership ability, and prospective vision make him a vital player in the contemporary business arena.

Michael holds degrees in both international business and real estate with a focus on commercial real estate development and finance. He credits over 20 years of competitive sailing with his father as the reason for his tactical and highly strategic approach to business structure, growth strategy, and leadership.

Originally from Delavan, Wisconsin, Michael now resides in Orlando, Florida.

Marc A. Price
Director of Operations, Expert Business Advice, LLC
Email: marc@expertbusinessadvice.com

Marc has collaborated with the Federal Government, United States Military, major non-profit organizations, and some of the largest corporations in America, developing and implementing new products, services and educational programs. Equally skilled in Business-to-Business and Business-to-Consumer functions, Marc has facilitated product positioning, branding and outreach efforts on many different platforms for the organizations he has worked with.

As an entrepreneur, Marc has successfully directed the launch of seven different companies, ranging from traditional brick-and-mortar establishments to innovative dot-com initiatives. Four were entertainment production companies (sound, lighting, staging, logistics, talent, entertainment), one was a business services company serving small companies, one was concerned with business and land acquisition, and two were website and business consulting services. Using his expertise in organizational management and small business development, Marc's latest focus is on working with new entrepreneurs and small-to-medium-sized businesses in emerging industries.

As an accomplished public speaker and writer, Marc has appeared on nationally syndicated television and radio networks, in national print publications, and has been the subject of numerous interviews and special-interest stories. Marc is a regular contributor to www.expertbusinessadvice.com.

Marc received his Bachelor of Science in Organizational Management from Ashford University. He and his wife divide time between Orlando, Florida and elsewhere, including an active schedule of international travel. His motto: "You can't build a reputation on what you are going to do."—Henry Ford

Mark R. Moon, Esq.

Email: MMoon@MoonLawGroup.com
Founder and Managing Attorney, Moon Law Group, P.L.

In 2009, Mark founded the Moon Law Group. His vision was to provide effective and educational legal services to individuals and small businesses by using technology and general business knowledge to create a new model of legal practice that is accessible and affordable to the average person and small business owner. Prior to founding the Moon Law Group, Mark was associate counsel in a large law firm specializing in the representation of banking institutions through their business and real estate operations in both state and federal jurisdictions. Before attending law school, Mark founded and operated a real estate sales and technology company. He also worked in the financial services sector, managing a branch location and earning his NASD series 6 and 7, Florida Real Estate, and Life, Health and Annuity licenses.

Mark earned his Bachelor of Science from the Warrington College of Business at the University of Florida, with Honors, majoring in Finance with a minor in Economics. He graduated from the Levin College of Law at the University of Florida, earning certificates in Estates, Trusts, Family and Elder law. Mark is currently admitted to practice in the State of Florida, the U.S. District Courts of Florida and the U.S. Court of Veterans' Appeals. He is a veteran of the U.S. Army and Operation Iraqi Freedom. Mark is a graduate of multiple military and business leadership courses.

Originally from Madeira Beach, Florida, Mark now lives in St. Petersburg, Florida with his wife and three children. His other work includes the growth of his firm, veteran-focused charity work and the advancement of the collaborative practice of law. His motto: "There is a problem: What are the solutions?"

Business Efficiency Resources

Get More Done Seminars

Grooms Consulting Group, a sister company to Nova Vista Publishing, offers proven training that saves professionals one month or more of time wasted on email, information and meeting inefficiency.

• 83% of all professionals are overloaded by email – we can save up to 3 weeks a year, per person
• 92% want to improve their information storage system – we can make searches 25% faster and more successful
• 43% of all meeting time is wasted – we can save up to another 3 weeks per year, per person

"We saved 15 days a year!"
Matt Koch, Director of Productivity
Capital One Financial Services

Three Two-Hour Modules: We offer three powerful seminars: **Get Control of Email, Get Control of Info**, and **Get Control of Meetings**.
They can be delivered in any combination you wish and can be customized.
Who Should Attend? Anyone who handles email, stores information, and attends meetings. Leaders leverage their position for added impact.
Delivery Options: Seminar, keynote speech, webinar, e-learning, and executive coaching.
Return on Investment (ROI): We can measure the impact of every session on participants with five-minute online pre- and post-surveys. We deliver a report that shows time saved, productivity gained, participant satisfaction, and other significant impacts.

Special pricing is available for groups.

Three *Get More Done* Modules: Combine and Customize as You Wish

1. GET CONTROL OF EMAIL
• Pump up your productivity by eliminating unnecessary email
• De-clutter your jammed inbox
• Write more effective messages
• Discover time-saving Outlook® / Lotus® tech tips
• Improve email etiquette and reduce legal liability
• Choose the best communication tool

2. GET CONTROL OF INFORMATION
• Get organized, once and for all
• Never lose a document again
• File and find your information in a flash; make shared drives productive
• Make better decisions with the right information
• Create an ordered, stress-free folder structure throughout your system

3. GET CONTROL OF MEETINGS
• Meet less and do more through virtual and other advanced options
• Reduce costs, boost productivity and go green with improved, efficient virtual meetings
• Run engaging, productive live meetings
• Discover time-saving e-calendar tips
• Keep every meeting productive and on track, make follow-ups easy

Satisfaction Guaranteed
We guarantee that the vast majority of your people will rate our seminars "excellent" or "good", or your money back.

"A huge hit with our people!"
Joel Burkholder
Regional Program Coordinator – ACLCP

Contact: Kathe Grooms
kgrooms@groomsgroup.com

Two Must-Read Books For Entrepreneurs

Time Out for Leaders: Daily Inspiration for Maximum Leadership Impact

Donald Luce and Brian McDermott

Leaders around the world recognize that daily reflection is absolutely necessary for defining values, establishing direction and pursuing vision. Luce and McDermott, two of the world's leading international consultants in leadership development, help leaders take ten minutes a day to focus on the principles they live by and help those around them develop and prosper.

In an attractive page-a-day format, each workday features a pithy quote, a reflection, and an action. A great gift for leaders you know, and for the leader in you.

"It is lonely at the top. Leaders can benefit from a daily dose of courage and values in Time Out for Leaders *and then approach their demanding tasks with renewed energy."*

Rosabeth Moss Kanter, Harvard Business School

Time Out for Leaders (ISBN for hardcover 978-9077256-10-7, ISBN for softcover 978-90-77256-30-6)
272 pages, 145 × 190 mm (5 ½" × 7")
Suggested retail price €19.95. $19.95 hardcover; €14.95, $14.95 softcover
Quote-a-day format; hardcover is jacketed with marker ribbon.

Social Styles Handbook: Adapt Your Style to Win Trust

Backed by a database of more than 2 million people, Wilson Learning's Social Styles concepts are powerful, life-changing communication tools. The ways people prefer to influence others and how they feel about showing emotion identify them as Analyticals, Expressives, Drivers or Amiables. You feel comfortable acting within your own style. But to relate to others well, you must consciously adjust your style to theirs. That's Versatility, which improves performance in every aspect of your work and life.

Find your style and learn to recognize others'. Understand and appreciate the strengths and differences in each. Learn how to become Versatile while still being yourself. Important tools for recognizing tension and Back-Up Behavior and handling it productively, plus techniques for influencing others, have made this a best-selling book that delivers results.

"I'm not sure I can quantify the value of using Social Styles, but I know I would not want to do my job without it."

Ann Horner, Main Board Director, Bourne Leisure Limited

Social Styles Handbook (ISBN Revised Edition 978-90-77256-33-6)
192 pages, softcover, 160 × 230 cm (6" × 9")
Suggested retail price: € 19.95, US$19.95
Models, charts, anecdotes, an index and other resources.

Now available in eBook formats!
www.novavistapub.com

CAREERS

I Just Love My Job!
Roy Calvert, Brian Durkin, Eugenio Grandi and Kevin Martin, in the Quarto Consulting Library (ISBN 978-90-77256-02-2, softcover, 192 pages, $19.95)

Taking Charge of Your Career
Leigh Bailey (ISBN 978-90-77256-13-8, softcover, 96 pages, $14.95)

LEADERSHIP AND INNOVATION

Grown-Up Leadership
Leigh Bailey and Maureen Bailey (ISBN 978-90-77256-09-1, softcover, 144 pages, $18.95)

Grown-Up Leadership Workbook
Leigh Bailey (ISBN 978-90-77256-15-2, softcover, 96 pages, $14.95)

Leading Innovation
Brian McDermott and Gerry Sexton (ISBN 978-90-77256-05-3, softcover, 160 pages, $18.95)

SALES

Win-Win Selling
Wilson Learning Library (ISBN 978-90-77256-34-3, softcover, 160 pages, $18.95)

Versatile Selling
Wilson Learning Library (ISBN 978-90-77256-03-2, softcover, 160 pages, $18.95)

Time Out for Salespeople
Nova Vista Publishing's Best Practices Editors, (ISBN 978-90-77256-14-5 hardcover with marker ribbon, 272 pages, $19.95; ISBN 978-90-77256-31-2 softcover, 272 pages, $14.95)

Get-Real Selling, Revised Edition
Michael Boland and Keith Hawk (ISBN 978-90-77256-32-9, softcover, 144 pages, $18.95)

SCIENCE PARKS, ECONOMICS, ECOLOGY OF INNOVATION

What Makes Silicon Valley Tick?
Tapan Munroe, Ph.D., with Mark Westwind, MPA (ISBN 978-90-77256-28-2, softcover, 192 pages, $19.95)

Visit www.novavistapub.com for sample chapters, reviews, links and ordering. eBooks are now available too!